David Bradshaw is one of [...] tual leaders I know. I have s[...] after year, even through the [...] because he practices the kin[...] of prayer he preaches. May his words inspire you to take up heaven's invitation to live in God's presence each day—now and always.

—HEIDI G. BAKER, PHD
COFOUNDER AND EXECUTIVE CHAIRMAN OF THE
BOARD, IRIS GLOBAL

A movement of day-and-night prayer, worship, and evangelism is touching college campuses and cities across the nation. David Bradshaw chronicles that movement in his book, *Awaken the Dawn*, but he does more than share the miraculous story of what God has done through the ministry he pioneered. David challenges us to become part of the same story—to discover how we can host Jesus' presence and introduce Him to those around us.

God is releasing various movements today that include prayer, worship, and missions that will be used by the Holy Spirit in releasing His transforming power to people, ministries, and various parts of cities and nations. Awaken the Dawn is one of these movements. He is sending an awakening to His church, even in these days, to prepare the body of Christ to reach the lost and impact the nations. And, as David writes, He will do this through people like you and me.

We have every reason to be hopeful that Jesus' leadership will be released and His beauty revealed and His name magnified. Stadiums will be filled, nations will be impacted, and churches will be revived to plant many new ones—and yes, miracles will be witnessed in an ever-increasing way in the coming days. I believe that this book will inspire God's people to discover their part in His great plan and to become part of the next great spiritual awakening.

—Mike Bickle
Founder, International House of Prayer of Kansas City

David Bradshaw is a catalytic voice to a generation. He lays out the cost that is commensurate to the outpouring. His painting what the Holy Spirit is doing every chapter culminates into the clear action before a generation.

—Brian Brennt
Cofounder, Circuit Riders;
Coleader, The Send Executive Team

I have had the wonderful privilege of personally watching David Bradshaw's story line unfold. It is a beautiful testimony of the move of God's Spirit in preparing the church for the coming of the Lord. Each chapter is filled with fascination, wisdom, and vision concerning the present global upper room being fashioned and the coming outpouring of the Holy Spirit upon all the nations for the fulfillment of the Great Commission and the salvation of Israel.

—Allen Hood
Director, Excellencies of Christ Ministries

I have known David personally for well over two decades. When I first met him, he was just sixteen years old. From the beginning there was one thing that stood out: he hungered relentlessly for God. What you hold in your hand is not merely theoretical or a collection of nice stories. The words penned by this man come from one who has persevered in faith and obedience through the furnace of adversity.

This book is an invitation from Jesus to radically alter your story line. It will give you the foretaste of what *could be* and the foresight for what *should be* in your life and community. I wholeheartedly endorse this book, *Awaken the Dawn*.

—BRIAN FRANCIS HUME
PROPHETIC MINISTER

ATD

AWAKEN
THE DAWN

AN ADVENTURE IN HOSTING JESUS' PRESENCE
AND DISCOVERING YOUR PART IN THE STORY

DAVID BRADSHAW

CHARISMA
HOUSE

Visit the author's website at https://awakenthedawn.com.

Library of Congress Cataloging-in-Publication Data:
An application to register this book for cataloging has been submitted to the Library of Congress.
International Standard Book Number: 978-1-63641-006-7
E-book ISBN: 978-1-63641-007-4

21 22 23 24 25 — 9 8 7 6 5 4 3 2 1
Printed in the United States of America

I dedicate this book to my amazing wife, Ashley, and my five children, Esther, Ezra, Jono, Heidi, and Hunter. Your sacrifice and love as we have walked out this journey of obedience to God as a family have been a great source of strength and life to me. There is no one I would rather journey with than you. Thank you for loving me and for your constant yes to Jesus. I look forward to all that God has for us together and for each of you as individuals. I am praying for you. The best is yet to come.

CONTENTS

INTRODUCTION

J ESUS IS THE most skilled of all writers.

He started crafting a grand drama even before creation, and it is unfolding in real time as we speak. His story is not exaggerated; it is full of wonder and designed to fascinate the imaginations and passions of those who are part of His family.

And amazingly you are part of the story.

A movement of day-and-night worship, prayer, creativity, and mission is impacting America and the nations by bringing the presence of God into our cities and campuses. This is God's blueprint for transformation, one clearly seen in Scripture. From David's tent in Jerusalem to the Upper Room on the day of Pentecost, the biblical narrative shows again and again that God's personal presence always changes everything.

Jesus is leading a procession of great awakening, which in the coming days, months, and years will fill stadiums, impact campuses, reach nations, and create an environment for miracles. This is what Jesus said He would do in Matthew 24:14: "This gospel of the kingdom will be preached in the whole world as a testimony to all nations, and then the end will come." And He is inviting you into the adventure.

I am convinced people and church communities who constantly interact with Jesus in worship and prayer are on the front lines of bringing God's dream to earth. In other words, God is raising up communities that host Jesus' presence as His primary strategy to bring change and justice. That includes you. He is calling you to join in the symphony of creative worship, prayer, and gospel proclamation that God is orchestrating. It is a miraculous story line that has your name in it, but you must embrace it. You won't live this adventure by accident.

The good news is that you don't have to strive to walk out your part in the story Jesus is writing. Some of my favorite verses on prayer are Isaiah 30:19–21. The prophet says, "He will surely be gracious to you at the sound of your cry. As soon as he hears it, he answers you....And your ears shall hear a word behind you, saying 'This is the way, walk in it,' when you turn to the right or when you turn to the left" (ESV).

This means that when you are praying as a lifestyle, God begins to move in your life, showing you, like a voice behind you, what your part is in the grand story Jesus is writing. It is not our job to do the heavy lifting in what God is asking us to do. All He is looking for is those who will give Him an unequivocal yes and stay in the conversation with Him. He does all the difficult (read: impossible!) work to accomplish His dream of transforming campuses, cities, and nations for His glory.

Jesus' way of changing the world is surprising and exhilarating and certainly the opposite of the systems of the world. In the pages that follow, I share just part of what happened when believers and church communities said yes to living out Jesus' story for their lives. We began to see God come near and transform hearts, lives, churches, cities, and even nations.

This is only the beginning. Jesus is still writing the story of how He brought awakening and transformation in the earth. And I pray that as you read what God has done so far, you will be inspired to discover the part you were made to play.

Whether you are in Gen Z (those born between 1997 and 2015) or a baby boomer, you were born for this hour. You will come alive when you know who you are and find your part in Jesus' plan. The adventure we've been on has been better than we could have ever imagined. May this book awaken your heart to the stunning joy of staying in a conversation with Jesus and seeing His presence fill your community and change everything.

PART I

LAUNCHING A MOVEMENT

Chapter 1

WHERE JESUS LIVES

My heart, O God, is steadfast; I will sing and
make music with all my soul. Awake, harp
and lyre! I will awaken the dawn.

—PSALM 108:1–2

I REMEMBER THE DAY vividly. It was 2003, and one of the leaders in the church where I served as a worship leader and youth pastor had just read a book called *Red Moon Rising*. In it, Pete Greig and Dave Roberts wrote about a 24/7 prayer movement that broke out in England and spread all over the world. Stirred by what she'd read, the leader suggested we consider praying 24/7 for a week in our church.

That sounded like the worst idea I had heard in a long time. For me, prayer was like going to the dentist. You only did it because you didn't want your teeth to fall out. You didn't spend extended hours in prayer out of any remote sense of enjoyment. Yes, good definitely would come of it. But to me, praying 24/7 for a full week sounded harder than manual labor.

But who can argue against prayer, right? So we agreed to pray 24/7 for three days because a week just seemed too long— and those three days changed my life forever.

The prayer meetings were like nothing I had ever experienced or even imagined. I knew what it was like for God to show up in a ministry gathering, but this was entirely different. We felt God's presence in a profound way, but it was not like a visitation in which God's presence marks a particular meeting. It was like God came to stay—day in and day out.

I was standing in the foyer on one of the days when a seventeen-year-old kid approached me and asked, "Can we never stop this?" The question resounded in my mind. Here was a teenager asking for 24/7 prayer to never stop. I wasn't the only one who was being forever changed.

A profound hunger for more was stirring in people's hearts, especially the youth. We sang at 3:00 a.m. We prayed our hearts out. We even had a DJ of sorts, and we danced and prayed for hours. We covered the walls with paper, and people wrote prayers and created artwork. Over the course of three days, a canvas of what God was doing in our midst was created as drawings, poems, and prayers covered the room.

Then something happened that really blew my mind. A young girl heard the sounds of our worship in the middle of the night and out of sheer curiosity wandered into the room off the street. She met Jesus that night. This was not what we had planned. Three days of 24/7 prayer wasn't designed to be an outreach. In my mind at the time, it was just a prayer gathering meant to prepare us for the real ministry that would come later. But people were coming to Jesus. And that young girl who committed her life to Jesus eventually ended up on the mission field.

I felt like I was stumbling into my calling, and I began to wonder if my idea of ministry was all wrong. What if instead of building our ministries and church communities only around meeting human needs, we built our communities around Jesus' presence and person? What if we made worship and prayer central to our churches and by extension made God's presence central? What if that is actually the best way to meet human needs because God is the ultimate answer to every problem we will ever face?

These may sound like nice goals, but they have proven to be some of the most disruptive ideas ever conceived—and some of the most fun to live out. Putting the presence of God and the lifestyle of worship at the center of church life forces us to trust God with the things we as humans would ordinarily assume control over. The lifestyle of worship and prayer causes us to be vulnerable to Jesus' heart and whatever He desires to do. It forces us to embrace His story over our own. It causes us to surrender our lives for His.

The most exciting adventures can only unfold when we make room for God to be who He is in all His creativity. When we said yes to the "boring" idea of hosting 24/7 prayer, we had no clue how very unboring our lives were going to become.

LIGHTNING STRIKES

Soon after our first experience of 24/7 prayer, we became addicts. We began doing 24/7 prayer events for weeks on end every few months. It was messy, loud, and real. They were just as much worship events as they were prayer events since as much of our time was spent singing as anything else. Music and prayer were always designed to flow in and out of each other (more on that later).

During the late-night shift of one of these early 24/7 prayer gatherings, something amazing happened as a handful of teenage girls were praying in the prayer room. It is amazing how little convincing it takes to get people to attend prayer gatherings when God is present.

In that 3:00 a.m. prayer meeting, hidden away in a tiny prayer room without fanfare and platforms, one of the girls had a vision of a lightning bolt striking and staying permanently in our city. God spoke to these girls that because of their prayers He was about to do something powerful that was going to have a lasting impact on our region. The permanent lightning bolt represented an ongoing move of God that was coming to Fredericksburg, Virginia, and these young girls had the audacity to believe that their voices directly contributed to its arrival. They began to pray in agreement with what they were hearing as they danced around the room in the middle of the night.

I woke up the next morning to a frantic phone call. *As the girls prayed, a lightning bolt struck the church!*

While they were praying about the vision of the permanent lightning bolt striking, actual lightning hit the building where they were. To all of our shock, the lightning bolt put a hole in the ceiling of the worship center right above the podium. We had to put a bucket on the platform to catch the rainwater.

Just days later, my friend Allen Hood from the International House of Prayer in Kansas City, Missouri, was visiting for a conference we had organized to mark the end of three weeks of 24/7 worship and prayer. He stood under the hole left in the ceiling when the lightning struck and spoke about Jesus and what it means to be a house of prayer. Suddenly, all across the room people started sobbing. I too was gripped by what the Holy Spirit was doing in the room. This was the permanent lightning bolt the girls had prayed about.

I knew at that time that nothing could stay the same.

I began dreaming about a generation, both young and old, discovering who they are in God, finding their voice through Him, and using it to influence the culture. I knew this mission was going to define my life. At that gathering, under the hole in the ceiling, I and hundreds of young adults were marked.

Soon phone calls and feedback started pouring in. One parent said that every time she asked her daughter what happened at the gathering, she would just start crying, as she was so overwhelmed by the love of Jesus. One group of youth who had been with us at the event went back to their hometown a few hours' drive from us. Three years later we were told they were still experiencing a move of God as a result of what God did when the "lightning" struck.

This was the stuff of dreams.

Is This Happening to Us?

Our church community developed a bit of a pattern. We would pray and sing 24/7 for several weeks, and annually at the end of one of those series of weeks we would invite as many young people as possible to a larger event. Each year the event was larger than the previous, and it became clear to us that God was up to something, as word of what was happening was beginning to spread.

We called these annual gatherings Awaken the Dawn from Psalm 108:1–3: "My heart, O God, is steadfast; I will sing and make music with all my soul. Awake, harp and lyre! I will awaken the dawn. I will praise you, LORD, among the nations; I will sing of you among the peoples." We dared to believe that being steadfast of heart and focusing on the one thing—intimacy with Jesus—would lead to an awakening. And that is exactly what we began to see.

On the final day of this particular three weeks of prayer, a teenage girl visited from Alabama. She had only one complete lung instead of two, and she was used to getting winded with any extended activity and definitely with any kind of exercise.

That night she began to dance in wild worship with the throngs of people. Suddenly she noticed that she could breathe in a way she had not been able to previously. She wasn't winded. She began to worship God more exuberantly than ever because she knew she had been healed. When she returned home, an X-ray revealed that God had indeed re-created her second lung. As she worshipped Jesus with her whole heart, God did something utterly impossible that she was not even asking for—He gave her a new lung. This riveted all our imaginations.

What else would God do if we would seek Him like this? Was it truly even possible to make this a lifestyle?

IT STARTED THIS WAY IN JERUSALEM

We were captivated by the thought that we could host the presence of Jesus—not just ideas about Him but the Holy Spirit powerfully revealing to us who Jesus actually is in a personal and tangible way. The presence of Jesus is Jesus—not a force or an atmosphere. We are interacting through the Holy Spirit with the same glorious person who walked the earth two thousand years ago, and He desires to do the same things in our cities and communities as He did then! This idea that God wants to dwell with church communities and in regions is not new, but I am convinced that communities that focus their time and best resources on seeking God's face in a culture of sustained prayer and worship will experience unique transformation. God will be central in all things. He will come into their midst. He will be everything.

This is how the first Jesus movement started. Two thousand years ago in Jerusalem, 120 likely young people were gathered in prayer in an Upper Room. Suddenly God rushed on them. Three thousand people were saved that day, and within about ten years or so, tens of thousands of people in Jerusalem were Jesus followers. Over and over, even after this revival on the day of Pentecost, these early believers went to the temple daily in prayer (Acts 2:46; 3:1). They were locked into a lifestyle of praying together. They developed a rhythm of meeting together to seek God, share new stories of what He had done, and do life together. And Jesus was the center of it all.

In fact Paul's great missionary movement to the Gentile world began the same way. Acts 13:2 says as they were "worshiping the Lord and fasting," the Holy Spirit spoke in the midst of this ongoing worship expression and launched Paul and Barnabas out on a missionary journey that was unlike anything the world had ever seen.

I have discovered from the Book of Acts that this pattern

is repeated many times, and it only continued. As Pete Greig writes in *Dirty Glory*:

> The pursuit of the presence of God has been, without exception or exaggeration, the prevailing passion and common purpose of all the saints in every generation since the time of Christ. Many of these women and men wrote great works, founded churches, fought cruel injustices, or made startling discoveries, but study their lives and you will quickly discover that the universal, all-consuming motivation that fuelled everything else they did was a desire for the presence of God.[1]

God is omnipresent, meaning He is everywhere, but there are times when His presence is tangible and palpably experienced. In these times, we are sensing God's proximity. God really does dwell with groups of people and in places, but I am now convinced that having God's manifest presence abide in our midst was never meant to be an occasional experience. It is meant to be our ongoing reality.

God is inviting us to break free from our spiritual hamster wheels of systemic religious activities that can cause us to mistakenly think God is present when we're really just hearing a lot of noise. Our ministry models and church programs have their places, but not at the expense of Jesus' presence. The great disrupter is calling us. He is calling everyday people to have a living, breathing conversation with the uncreated One in which we not only speak but we hear back from Him. That may sound like a mental illness to some but not to the saints, not to those who are committed to hosting Jesus' presence so He can abide in our college campuses, church communities, cities, and nations.

Chapter 2

THE INSANITY OF DAVID

One thing I have desired of the LORD, that will I seek: that I may dwell in the house of the LORD all the days of my life, to behold the beauty of the LORD, and to inquire in His temple.

—PSALM 27:4, NKJV

DAVID WAS KING of Israel about three thousand years ago, but he was also one of the greatest pioneers of hosting the presence of God. No one had ever talked about God the way David did. What David said in Psalm 27:4 was one of the most amazing statements ever articulated by a human being about God. This posture defined his life, and it is in fact why God plucked David from tending sheep in his father's field to become Israel's second king.

David valued the presence of God above everything else. This desire found expression in his daily life and became the primary paradigm through which he ran his government. The significance of David's passion for God cannot be overstated.

David was a worshipper before anything else. The essence of worship is to value and pursue one thing: the presence of God and a profound intimacy with Him in that place.

It is Jesus plus nothing. Anything else is idolatry.

Worship reflects a love for God at the heart level and a passion to see Him exalted above all else—even oneself. David's worshipful heart caught God's eye more than his giftedness, qualifications, or accomplishments. This heart posture still catches God's eye.

This dream of David's heart to live in the presence of God was not simply one item on a list of desires. It was an all-consuming focus that surpassed every other desire. His passion was so peculiar that even David's own family misunderstood him.

I can feel the pain in David's words when he said he was like "a foreigner to my own family, a stranger to my own mother's children; for zeal for your house [God's presence] consumes me" (Ps. 69:8–9). He even said, "The drunkards make songs about me" (Ps. 69:12, ESV). Imagine that. Drunkards sang about David because his zeal for God's presence was so evident to everyone around him.

Some people are known primarily for their political aspirations, their natural giftedness, or any number of positive attributes. But David was marked by his pursuit of God's presence; it was the very essence of who he was and determined how he ordered his life. Some people thought he was crazy, but in reality he was the sanest of all people. Insanity is to lack awe in the presence of endless beauty.

What if you discovered that a billion dollars was buried under your house and whoever dug it up could have it? What would sanity look like in that situation? You would grab a pickax and start to dig through your floor! To passersby, it might look as if you had lost your mind. But if they knew what you knew, they might grab a shovel and start digging themselves, hoping to get even a little of the treasure for themselves.

David knew something most of us, even many of us who quote his psalms frequently, don't seem to know concerning how to live when no one is watching. He knew he had real access to the essence of happiness and power in his very personal and intimate relationship with God.

This lifestyle focused on the presence of God was the secret to David's life, success in his calling, and personal transformation. It is the same for us. The mystery is that we cannot change ourselves, but when we behold God as He is (read: experience His presence in our lives), we are transformed. This is what Paul taught us about a thousand years after David modeled this life:

> But we all, with unveiled face, beholding as in a mirror
> the glory of the Lord, are being transformed into the
> same image from glory to glory, just as by the Spirit
> of the Lord.
>
> —2 CORINTHIANS 3:18, NKJV

There is a certain wildness about the way David worshipped and lived. What gripped David couldn't be further from stoic religious moralism, but it also was not the kind of dangerous passion you see in some religious environments. That kind of self-destructive zeal is not love for God at all; rather it is rooted in a prideful attempt to gain God's love through one's own abilities or activities.

David's passion was something altogether different. It was worship. It was what C. S. Lewis described in *The Weight of Glory*:

> It would seem that Our Lord finds our desires not too strong, but too weak. We are half-hearted creatures, fooling about with drink and sex and ambition when infinite joy is offered us, like an ignorant child who wants to go on making mud pies in a slum because he cannot imagine what is meant by the offer of a holiday at the sea. We are far too easily pleased.[1]

To love God as David did isn't extreme; it actually makes you healthier. You become a better friend, a better spouse, a better person when your focus is on the "one thing." Most things in life we can love too much or, better said, in the wrong way, but there is one obsessive love that is not unhealthy at all. The more obsessive it becomes, the more we are healed, joyful, and reasonable with others. In fact it is how we become truly and fully alive. As Kevin Prosch brilliantly wrote in his song "Endlessness," "There is no danger in the excess of loving You."[2]

Though he lived thousands of years ago, David is the model

of the all-consuming love God is looking for in us. I believe it is because of his central value for intimacy with God that David was chosen to produce the lineage of Jesus. Jesus is called the Son of David. This is more than a natural heritage.

The desire that moved David's heart didn't originate with David. It was Jesus' desire. Jesus Himself said, "Father, I desire that they also, whom you have given me, may be with me where I am, to see my glory" (John 17:24, ESV). The passion for God to dwell tangibly with us is the passion of the Trinity. We have seen only the beginning of this love affair that is going to grip the church across the nations.

AFTER GOD'S HEART

When David came along, Israel had already gotten a taste of life with a human king at the helm. Saul, Israel's first king ever and David's immediate predecessor, had everything a king should have. He was what the people asked for: smart, good-looking, wealthy, and an amazing military leader. But at his core Saul was narcissistic and arrogant instead of God obsessed. In short he was the exact opposite of a worshipper.

Consider the following passage:

> So [Saul] said, "Bring me the burnt offering and the fellowship offerings." And Saul offered up the burnt offering. Just as he finished making the offering, Samuel arrived, and Saul went out to greet him.
>
> "What have you done?" asked Samuel.
>
> Saul replied, "When I saw that the men were scattering...I felt compelled to offer the burnt offering."
>
> "You have done a foolish thing," Samuel said. "You have not kept the command the LORD your God gave you; if you had, he would have established your kingdom over Israel for all time. But now your kingdom will not endure; the LORD has sought out a

man after his own heart and appointed him ruler of
his people."

—1 SAMUEL 13:9–14

Saul actually used the priesthood of Israel as a means of
securing his place in leadership instead of to sincerely express
his love to God. Let that sink in for a minute. Saul sought to use
the presence of God for selfish reasons and to prevent personal
loss. This was Saul's great test, and he failed. His army was out-
numbered by more than ten to one against the Philistines, and
he resorted to reliance on fleshly wisdom and self-preservation
instead of obeying the word of God given through Samuel and
waiting to make a sacrifice to the Lord the correct way. This is
the same test leaders are facing to this day! Will we seek God's
face and lean on Him or press forward in our own strength?

Now notice who God selected as Saul's replacement: David, a
man after God's own heart. This means David was focused on
authentically knowing God and how He felt above his desire for
position or power.

To this day, God is looking for this very thing: "The LORD
does not look at the things people look at. People look at the
outward appearance, but the LORD looks at the heart" (1 Sam.
16:7). Long before Samuel recognized David as the next king of
Israel, God had already discovered him, even though outwardly
David was not even in the running. In fact David could not
have been more hidden. God really does not look at the outward appearance. But believe me, God is looking at my heart
and yours.

WEAK, NOT STRONG

Perhaps you are like me when you read about the life of David,
and his story makes you aware of your lack of this kind of
desire for God. I have often said that prayer is at the same time
the most exciting part of the Christian life and the most boring.

Netflix is so much more accessible than God's presence, it seems. The good news is that even weak pursuit of God counts as sincere. Weak love is still real love to God, and expressing it only makes it grow stronger.

David had father issues like many of us. In fact some scholars believe he was an illegitimate child of Jesse since he said that "in sin my mother conceived me" (Ps. 51:5, NKJV). When the greatest prophet in the world came to visit, David's dad didn't even send for him along with his other sons. When David finally found a spiritual father in King Saul, he ended up running from him for years in fear of his life because Saul was jealous of him.

What's more, David seriously messed up—he more than messed up. He sinned on such a grand level, some would say he had gone too far for any amount of grace. He slept with a married woman who was not his wife and had her husband killed. Not only that, this woman's husband had faithfully served David in his army. If any of us sin in such a way, we may sink into a pit of shame. We may run from God. But David didn't run from God. He ran *to* God.

David is not just a model in his zeal for God, but he is also a model of how God deals in kindness with weak people who turn to Him with their whole hearts. You don't have to be strong to live a "one thing" life; you just have to keep pursuing Him with a sincere heart. The key is to never give up.

David's Tent

At some point in his journey, David took a vow that changed the world. He vowed that he would not give himself a comfortable life until God was living in Jerusalem. He took his pursuit of the presence of God beyond where most of us would ever be comfortable.

> [David] swore an oath to the LORD, he made a vow to
> the Mighty One of Jacob: "I will not enter my house
> or go to my bed, I will allow no sleep to my eyes or
> slumber to my eyelids, till I find a place for the LORD,
> a dwelling for the Mighty One of Jacob."
>
> —PSALM 132:2–5

David understood that he wasn't the only one who needed
the presence of God near; God's presence was needed in communities and even nations. David's vow informed all his leadership decisions as king and thus changed the trajectory of the
whole world. David was not content with just having a decent
personal prayer life. He wanted God's presence to be revealed
in all of Israel and even all the earth. This is still God's heart.
Jesus wants to come and live in cities and church communities. He wants to find communities where He can show up and
show off.

When David finally became king of all of Israel and set up
his capital in Jerusalem, his first initiative was to find the ark of
the covenant, the golden box that represented God's personal
presence. When he located it, David brought it to Jerusalem, set
it in a tent, and hired four thousand musicians and 288 singers
to worship in that tent 24/7 (1 Chron. 23:5; 25:7). In doing this,
David surrounded the ark with 24/7 worship and put it right in
the center of the nation of Israel.

The worship around the tent went on for over thirty years.
This wasn't something the Law specifically told David to do.
This came largely from the overflow of his heart and probably
from some key conversations with Samuel, the great prophet.

But I am convinced that David was also a pragmatist. He
knew what would happen if unceasing worship filled Jerusalem.
David is the one who said God dwells in the praises of His
people (Ps. 22:3). Knowing God's presence changes everything,

David would have realized that nothing could be more practical than having God's presence in the heart of Jerusalem.

Imagine the conversation David inevitably had with his team about his decision to pitch the tent and hire the musicians to worship 24/7. Paying thousands of musicians and preparing for the temple to be built would cost hundreds of millions of dollars, and I am sure someone in David's administration objected strongly to the sheer extravagance of this expense. Here is an amazing fact, though, that proves David was a genius. Every time David's worship movement was restored in Israel's history, the nation began to prosper, and every time Israel backslid from this focus, they fell into crisis.

David's tent is not widely understood, but David's establishing 24/7 worship around God's presence was one of his most important decisions. And just think, God says in Acts 15:16 that He is going to restore David's tent. This verse refers to God's restoring David's kingdom through Jesus, but I believe it also points to the passion for worship at the core of David's government and his literal tent-filled 24/7 worship. When David created a place for God's presence and filled it with unbroken worship, heaven came down. God set His throne in an environment surrounded by worship and love songs.

The uniqueness of the worship renaissance in David's tabernacle was something that David received by revelation (2 Chron. 29:25). Somehow David was seeing and replicating worship in heaven. God's throne is surrounded with 24/7 worship, prayers, color, light, and love (Rev. 4–5). So when we pray for God's will to be done "on earth as it is in heaven," as Jesus taught in the Lord's Prayer (Matt. 6:9–13), we must understand that we're praying for a movement of worship and prayer, because intimacy with God is at the core of heaven. God longs for intimacy and interaction with us in the most personal way, and He set up His government to function this way. There are things God will do only when we are talking and singing to Him.

God chose this culture of unceasing worship and prayer to execute His will, and He still chooses worship and prayer as the context within which to uniquely show Himself. Heaven actually comes down to earth when we create a lifestyle of prayer and worship. And when that happens, things down here will become like things up there.

What David understood is that in the midst of unceasing worship, God's presence lived in a unique way—and God's presence changes everything. He knew that when God was present, it would affect every aspect of Israel's culture, including its economics, defense, and relationships.

So even to this day, making dynamic and passionate pursuit of Jesus' presence the center of how we do life together is not a selfish quest for an experience for an experience's sake. Rather it is a living interaction with the One who can change our hearts and our communities forever. Like David we pursue Jesus not for selfish reasons but as a means to serve and love others. Jesus is still saving, healing, and transforming people and communities!

PRAYER IS NOT ABOUT PRAYER

When we gathered all those years ago for those first three days of 24/7 prayer, we were not gathering around the activity of prayer or worship. Prayer is not about prayer. We pray because we believe in the One we are speaking to and that He loves to answer us. We believe He moves at the sound of our voices. As soon as prayer becomes about prayer and we forget that we are talking to an actual person—the One with eyes like blazing fire (Rev. 19:12)—we've lost the plot.

If the church is to be known for more than marketing campaigns and hollow and (dare I say it) boring church services, if we are going to be more than a cult of personality, if we are going to have joy that is stronger than all our addictions, we need to recover David's passion for God Himself to be the main attraction. May it become like a living flame in our thoughts and hearts and all our strategic planning.

So you see, launching prayer rooms is not the primary goal—though many prayer rooms will be launched. Even the external expression of worship is not truly our aim if it's centered around a personality or event. I live in a nation that has put millions of dollars into reaching the next generation. We have massive marketing campaigns, but they are just not enough. Love is what we need. But love has a name. It is a living person we need.

We need more than moralistic and political messages. We need Christ Himself to become the main focus of our talks and the center of our lives. When that happens, prayer, worship, and gospel proclamation movements are going to crescendo, and Jesus' presence is going to abide in campuses, cities, regions, and even nations.

The Jesus movement that began two thousand years ago has not been canceled. We can live the same adventure. The world is waiting.

Chapter 3

FROM EVENTS TO A LIFESTYLE

We regard [prayer] no longer as a duty that must be performed, but rather as a privilege that is to be enjoyed, a rare delight that is always revealing some new beauty.

—E. M. Bounds

WE SCHEDULED ANOTHER three weeks of 24/7 prayer in early 2008. What we didn't know is that this was going to be different from any of the other prayer events we had done.

Before the weeks of prayer were to begin, my father, Scott Bradshaw, whose walk with God has impacted me more than anyone else's, had a dream. In the dream a man came to him with a blueprint. When he took the blueprint from the man, he saw that it depicted a new structure. Several times in the dream my dad handed the blueprint back to the man and the man gave it back to him, and each time when Dad unrolled the blueprint, he discovered the structure had grown and changed. The third time they made this exchange, the actual presence of God filled the structure. Dad knew from the dream that God was about to start something new. The trouble was that we were not exactly looking to start something entirely new.

So we started our twenty-one days of 24/7 prayer. The very first night, a friend named Kirk Bennett came to speak to our church community. "These three weeks of prayer are going to birth a new expression of day-and-night prayer in your region," he said.

I didn't know if I believed him because we were quite comfortable doing what we were doing. We had already been praying like this for a few years now. So what was supposed to change?

The issue is that when you are going after God in prayer for lengths of time, anything can happen. It was like we were riding a wave of prayer and desire for God to show Himself in our community of believers. Some places are irresistible to God. We had become a bit like that but didn't really appreciate that God was about to respond to us in a big way.

BIRTHED, NOT STARTED

What happened during those twenty-one days is unlike anything I've ever experienced before or since. For twenty-one days, day and night, our small group of mostly young people found ourselves in a kind of supernatural travail that was beyond anything I had known. It was amazing and glorious. I had heard of this kind of thing before. Romans 8:26 speaks of the Holy Spirit interceding for us "with groanings too deep for words" (ESV), and that's what was happening. We were travailing with tears for God to dwell in our city and for justice to come. God was there, and after years of prayer something was being birthed supernaturally.

We love to present ourselves to those around us as if we have things figured out. We love our well-put-together moments. But often it is our tears that define us. Pay attention to what you weep over; it just might reveal your calling.

There is nothing wrong with planning events and using wisdom to organize them. But the movements Jesus orchestrates are birthed, not just planned. It is important to go to a boardroom and develop a strategic plan using common sense and wisdom, but things that are being launched by the Holy Spirit often can't be controlled and don't start simply in a boardroom. They start in a supernatural interaction with Jesus—in a life of praying, listening, and believing.

As the days went by, the intensity of our travail seemed to only get stronger, and I found myself wondering where this was going. I looked around the room to see some of my closest friends with their eyes closed and tears streaming down their faces, as if they had forgotten about everything but Jesus. Day after day this persisted for three weeks.

On the very last day of the three weeks, I was lying on the floor of our little prayer room, my face soaked with tears. It was like a wrecking ball had hit the room. I heard the door open, and a missionary friend walked in. She was fresh from Africa, where she had been working with Heidi Baker's ministry.

"This twenty-one-day fast is birthing a new prayer community," she said almost immediately.

I managed to look up to see who was speaking. I hadn't believed Kirk Bennett when he spoke those very words on day one of our twenty-one days, but to hear my friend say the very same thing on the last of the twenty-one days was like a confirmation beyond a doubt.

This must have been the blueprint in my dad's dream. The great disrupter had walked into our lives and invited us into something beyond us.

I've found this often happens when you desire to walk out Jesus' story for your life. God doesn't want us to get comfortable in our past breakthroughs. I wasn't fully aware of it at the time, but I had been growing comfortable. I had a good job at the church. We had established a comfortable rhythm of 24/7 prayer and were doing many good things in ministry. But good can be the enemy of God's best, and He loves to pry us loose so we don't miss His best.

Sometimes it takes years or even decades for God's plans and purposes to unfold. But when the shift comes, it can be fast and disorienting. This just forces us to lean into God. When we are weak, He is strong. God excels at keeping us slightly off balance—at least in the way we perceive things—so He can be our everything.

A few months after that season of travail, I understood what new thing God wanted us to do. He sent me and a small team out from our church to launch a day-and-night worship and prayer room then known as the Prayer Furnace. To our knowledge, there had never been nonstop worship and prayer like this in our region. We were hungry. We wanted to say yes to God, however messy, weak, and imperfect we were at times (and we were all those things). Looking back now, we learned much and made many mistakes on this journey, but God has been faithful to move even in our weakness.

As we prayed and worshipped in the little prayer room we'd found, there were times when heaven seemed to be so close. It went beyond our wildest expectations. We were in shock and awe of God. Numerous times, I would be sitting in a meeting of some kind, and I'd get a text message saying, "Come to the prayer room immediately! God is doing something incredible!" I would run over to the prayer room to find scores of people undone in God's presence, and stories of healings and miracles began to stack up. Some of the people who now work with Awaken the Dawn initially showed up in the prayer room as addicted and bored young people and were transformed.

As I was writing this chapter, I was reminded of something wholly supernatural that happened during this season. Two people from India visited the prayer room. They were overwhelmed by Jesus' love for them, but neither spoke much English. Well, there just happened to be someone in the prayer room from the exact region of India they were from who spoke their exact dialect. Because God orchestrated the perfect timing of their meeting in that prayer room, we were able to communicate the gospel to them, and the two met God that day. God is so near!

Located at what is now our Awaken the Dawn base in Fredericksburg, that room has hosted prayer and worship for over ten years now. Through the years different seasons have brought different hours of daily prayer in our prayer room—sometimes we've gone twenty-four hours a day, some-times twelve hours a day, and sometimes just a few hours a day, but we have learned so much in the process. We've learned that no matter what our yes to the Lord looks like, Jesus has been near, and everything God has done in our lives and ministry has flowed out of that intimacy.

That's what God wants to do in each of us. He wants us to host His presence so that out of our intimacy with Him, His love and power will flow out from us to the world around us on a daily basis. This kind of intimacy is our birthright, but we won't walk in its fullness unless we understand who we are.

WE ARE PRIESTS

After we launched the Prayer Furnace, I gave myself full-time to what God called me to, trusting Him for financial provision for my young, growing family and our community of over one hundred people. We knew we wanted to see a Jesus movement in our nation and around the world. We knew God was doing something that was much bigger than just our little prayer room. But instead of showing us all He had in store, God began to lead us into a deeper understanding of our identity. God seems to always circle back to our hearts, if you haven't noticed already.

One passage that rocked us as it developed our under-standing of who we are in God is Revelation 1:5–6: "To him who loves us and has freed us from our sins by his blood, and has made us to be a kingdom and priests to serve his God and Father." This is not some bizarre statement; this is our actual calling. We are priests and kings. This means God is not going to accomplish what He wants to do on the earth without us. What we are doing in prayer and obedience to Jesus has cosmic significance, and that is not hype.

What does it mean to be a priest? I can tell you what it does not mean. It does not mean we wear robes and kill animals, as the priests did in the Book of Leviticus. Actually those sacrifices were a foreshadowing of what Jesus would accomplish on the cross, becoming the sacrifice for our sins through His death and thus giving us access to God. Looking at the priests' lives tells us something about our lives. Hebrews speaks of these priests and their work as "a shadow of the good things that are coming" (Heb. 10:1).

The passage in Revelation says Jesus died not just to forgive us but to make us priests, so this role must be pretty important. To be a priest means you have direct access to God in prayer and you can hear His voice. The priests in the Old Testament were given access to the very presence of God. When Jesus died, the curtain that separated everyone but the priests from God's presence ripped. So now all God's children have even greater access than the priests of old did. We have access to God's presence, activity, and goodness.

Just as eagles were made to soar, you were made for a life far beyond your wildest imagination. Jesus died to give you unparalleled access to God, yet many are living beneath what is already theirs! So I want to share four truths about what being a priest of God reveals about who you are and how God designed you to function.

1. You Have Total Access

As a priest of God you now have complete access to talk with and encounter God at any time and in any place without hindrance. We don't always feel that, but it is real. In fact, because the Holy Spirit lives in you, you are able to access even God's thoughts as you learn to hear Him in your heart. You cannot relate to God this way and remain unchanged. It affects everyone and everything around you. Once you taste this life of intimacy with Jesus, things that used to matter a great deal to you will begin to fade into the background and become almost obsolete.

I first met Heidi Baker, the great missionary in Mozambique and beyond, in Washington, DC. I was part of a small group that picked her up from the airport when she was in town for a conference, and we immediately stopped at an Italian restaurant for dinner. Almost as soon as we sat down, a server approached us to take our orders. We had not been talking about anything spiritual. We were giving our drink orders, and the server turned to Heidi and suddenly froze.

"Are you a minister?" she asked.

Heidi smiled and replied, "Oh, you see Jesus in me."

What struck me was that we had not said anything about Jesus. That woman felt the nearness of God because Heidi was carrying His presence.

Before I knew it, it was like revival broke out in the restaurant. The woman was crying. People were praying. And I was thinking, "How did this happen before Heidi had even spoken a word?" Heidi had the fragrance of Jesus' presence on her life, and it literally changed the atmosphere of that little Italian restaurant. Most importantly it impacted that woman forever.

This is what happens when we draw near to God as a lifestyle. Peter's shadow healed people as he walked down the road (Acts 5:15–16). That power came out of Peter's personal communion with the Holy Spirit, and the same power is available to you and me as we access God's presence.

This is not necessarily about hosting more events or large gatherings or church meetings. We are called to experience intimacy with Christ throughout the day and in our dreams at night. God gives us a hidden life that will be filled with stories of how He is speaking to, meeting, and encountering us personally.

Meeting with Jesus is your first and main calling. Everything you are called to do comes from the inside out. You are no longer doing things for God. You are doing things with God. At its core this secret life is simply talking to God and hearing Him through the Bible and prayer. But it is a supernatural journey.

Perhaps as you read this, a new desire for God is stirring in your heart. That is because these words are touching your identity. You have settled for so much less than you have access to. It's time to draw close to God as a lifestyle. It is the normal Christian (priestly) life to have new stories of what the Holy Spirit is doing in and around you on a weekly basis. The stories won't always be as dramatic as people getting healed as your shadow passes by, but they will attest to the fact that you are a priest who has the right of full access to the presence of God. It is time to stretch your wings and soar into the lifelong journey of making intimacy with Jesus your primary focus.

2. You Are a Worshipper

Second, as priests, worship is our main vocation. We worship not because God needs us to do so. We worship because He desires to spend time with us and we become our truest selves when we are living with eyes for Him alone—when we are sensitized to the presence of Jesus and can see what God is doing.

I believe God is looking for leaders who will make their ministry to God—their time worshipping and encountering Him—their primary focus. Everything else must be second. Jesus said, "Seek first his kingdom and his righteousness, and all these things will be given to you as well" (Matt. 6:33).

Praising and worshipping God are the consummation of our enjoyment of God. Think about it this way. If you were driving by a beautiful mountain landscape and someone was in the car with you, to really enjoy what that beautiful landscape represents, you as a human are almost compelled to turn to the other person and say, "Look at that. It's amazing." That is praise. God says to worship Him not because He is narcissistic but because He is the best and the most beautiful—far more beautiful than anything you could even imagine. He is so stunning that angels can cry out, "Holy," all day and night without a moment of boredom.

As John Piper says:

> Praising God, the highest calling of humanity and our eternal vocation, did not involve the renunciation but rather the consummation of the joy I so desired. My old effort to achieve worship with no self-interest in it proved to be a contradiction in terms. Worship is basically adoration, and we adore only what delights us. There is no such thing as sad adoration or unhappy praise. We have a name for those who try to praise when they have no pleasure in the object. We call them hypocrites.[1]

You won't be fully yourself or fulfill your purpose without being a worshipper before all else. Some kinds of ministries will go away one day; for instance, missions won't be necessary after the new heaven and earth are established. But worship is never ever going to end.

Everyone is naturally a worshipper. We cannot stop worshipping any more than we can stop breathing. We worship what we enjoy most in life and the things in which we place our deepest trust. The question is, Just what do we look to as our source of joy and confidence? For God to instruct us to worship Him is for Him to instruct us to be our truest selves.

The reality of worship is that it does not change just the atmosphere around us; it changes us because we become what we behold (2 Cor. 3:18). Time and exposure to the presence of God will progressively change our emotions and can even heal our physical bodies.

There are many times when you worship and don't feel

it deeply in the moment, but you worship anyway. In fact, if you worship long enough by faith, your feelings will follow. Authentic worship isn't a song; it is to give God your attention, love, and trust above all things.

God is not seeking worship. He is seeking worshippers (John 4:23). This is because you are your truest self when you are a worshipper. As we worship, using music and the arts especially, we will increasingly host Jesus' presence because the more we praise Him, the more we see of Him, and the more we see of Him, the more we will want to worship.

3. You Are an Intercessor

Third, being a priest means you get to be an intercessor. This means we talk to God about others, and He moves in response to our voices and changes things in real time.

I know a leader who years ago had a vivid dream. In the dream he saw five doors. Written over each of the five doors were the leadership roles described in Ephesians 4:11—apostle, prophet, pastor, teacher, and evangelist.

There were long lines of people trying to get through each door and jostling with one another to stand in the place of influence these doors represented. There were so many people in those lines that this minister knew he could never get through the doors. The path was way too crowded.

Then he turned to one side and saw two other doors. Written over one door was the word *intercessor* and over the other door was the word *servant*. It seemed these two were the unpopular doors because no one was lining up to go through them, so he entered the intercessor door.

To his amazement, on the other side of the door were five more doors. The words *apostle, prophet, pastor, teacher,* and *evangelist* were written over the doors, one word over each door. This time, there was no line.

This is the secret to becoming an influencer as God defines it. You go through the intercessor door, which means you make praying for and serving others your main focus, and you will step into the influence and leadership God endorses with His favor.

I've always thought it a bit strange when we talk about worshippers and intercessors as if they are some special category of human being or unique ministries in and of themselves. I admit, some are more called to these expressions than others in terms of how much time they devote to them. But everyone is called to be a worshipper, and everyone is called to be an intercessor. Why? Because authority comes from intimacy, and we are all called to walk in kingdom authority.

I will go further. There is no real lasting influence or authority in Jesus' kingdom without being a lover of God and an intercessor for others. This shifts us from a focus on events to a lifestyle of intimacy with Jesus. It means we are more focused on things that are unseen than what we can see with our natural eyes, yet we are more relevant than ever to the culture around us.

Let's consider heaven for a minute. In the Book of Revelation the primary leaders are seen seated with God. These are actually human beings, as we see in Revelation 5:

> He went and took the scroll from the right hand of
> him who sat on the throne. And when he had taken it,
> the four living creatures and the twenty-four elders fell
> down before the Lamb. Each one had a harp and they
> were holding golden bowls full of incense, which are
> the prayers of God's people.
>
> —Revelation 5:7–8

This passage tells us the leadership team with Jesus—the elders—all have two things in their hands. They have a musical instrument in one hand and a bowl filled with our prayers in the other hand. Think about what kind of leadership model this represents. The top leaders in heaven are playing music and involved in prayer!

Imagine if, when the US Congress was in session, all the senators and representatives were required to bring guitars and each session had to open with extended times of singing. We would think they had finally lost it. What government is run this way? Jesus' kingdom works this way, and it frustrates the world.

Kings were known for their external accomplishments, but priests were known for their lifestyles. Again, intercession isn't some boring ritual we have to participate in—we *get to* pray.

4. You Are a Messenger

Lastly, being a priest means you are also a messenger from God to people. When you draw near to Jesus, you become filled with Him. Then you become a voice rather than an echo. Your life begins to shout about what Jesus is really like and what He is saying, and God's words lead us to action. The voice of God always brings change.

One of my spiritual fathers is a man named Bowie Curry. He came to Jesus in the 1970s when he was on his way to South America in a VW bus with a guru. Their plan was to run around naked during the summer solstice. After a disagreement through which Bowie realized the guru was a fake, he was left stranded on the side of the road. It was there on the side of the road that Bowie called on Jesus and was instantly filled with a peace he had never experienced before.

Shortly after this time, he decided to go to a Bible school in the middle of the desert in the southwestern United States. At this school the students would spend the first part of every day in silent prayer. Bowie was bewildered. He had no idea what to do. All the students would simply sit silently with God. Finally

Bowie drummed up the courage to ask someone what was going on.

"Just find a verse from the Bible, picture it in your mind, and ask God to reveal more of what He is saying through the passage," someone told him.

This seemed to be such a strange thing to do. But Bowie had come all the way to this Bible school and figured he should give this a try. He decided to read Psalm 23. Every day he would read Psalm 23 and spend time prayerfully pondering this chapter. The first verse says, "The LORD is my shepherd, I lack nothing." Bowie would meditate on this psalm over and over again.

Soon he began to experience God's nearness. The psalm came alive. God began to speak to him. Before long Bowie was skipping meals to spend more time in the prayer room. He had made the great discovery of his access to God!

It was around this time that the students went on an outreach to a maximum-security prison. Bowie was given a period of time with one of the inmates in the facility. He wondered what a young man like him would share with someone in prison. How could he love an inmate well in the midst of his situation?

Bowie did the only thing he could think to do. He began to share what had been happening to him in the prayer room. He shared out of Psalm 23. To Bowie's surprise he looked up to find the inmate sobbing. This man was experiencing God as Bowie spoke out of what he encountered with Jesus. The Holy Spirit had come into the prison.

Soon other inmates began to crowd around to hear Bowie talk. They were transfixed. This young man who had been sitting with Jesus for weeks suddenly had authority that was perhaps more powerful than what a lot of preachers we hear carry. We become messengers with our words, songs, and lives when we access Jesus' presence and stay in the conversation with Him as a lifestyle! We can all become authentic influencers in the way God defines the concept as we walk in intimacy with Jesus. It is guaranteed. History makers are priests of Jesus.

Your Prayer Adventure

You may be wondering how to make this adventure in prayer and worship a reality in your life. How do you begin to host God's presence in your home, in your church community, on your campus, in your city?

One of the most helpful and practical tools I have found to develop a lifestyle of prayer and worship is to use a prayer list and commit to a regular schedule of personal prayer. Doing this has been revolutionary in my life. You can create your own list; you don't have to use the same list your pastor or favorite minister is using.

Your list may start with five or six items and grow to fifteen to twenty points or more. You might end up with multiple prayer lists. The key is that you write it down and that you include three types of prayers: those focused on adoring Jesus for who He is, devotional prayers about your personal needs or desires, and prayers for others or justice. If you're having trouble discerning how to pray for your own needs, ask yourself, What am I seeking God for? What is my life vision?

Once you've developed your list, find scriptures that apply to each prayer point. You will end up memorizing these verses; you may even use these passages as language for your prayers. Praying the Scriptures is powerful because God's Word is His will, and when we pray according to His will, we know He will answer (1 John 5:14).

In the appendix I have included a prayer list Mike Bickle developed using the acronym FELLOWSHIP. This list is focused on prayer to strengthen the inner man, or what some call devotional prayer, but I have found this to be very helpful and have used it myself many times.

Every time you spend time in prayer, you can orient yourself around your list. You can spend as little or as much time on each point as you feel God leading. It is not meant to be strict. Sometimes you may end up not even using this list in prayer. But having it as a reference point can be life changing. You'll not only see God answer your prayers, but also new dreams and passions will begin to unfold.

Chapter 4

PORTABLE TOILETS AND HOT DOG STANDS

Hearing God is not all that difficult. If we know the Lord, we have already heard His voice—after all, it was the inner leading that brought us to Him in the first place. But we can hear His voice once and still miss His best if we don't keep on listening. After the *what* of guidance come the *when* and the *how*.

—LOREN CUNNINGHAM, *IS THAT REALLY YOU, GOD?*

As I MENTIONED previously, our annual gatherings were getting larger and larger until they eventually drew thousands of young people to Fredericksburg. When we began planning our 2009 event, we knew none of the venues we had previously used would work, so we started praying about a location, and I had a dream in which we were using a massive circus tent.

The person who owned the tent was a man named Neil, and he lived in North Carolina. I did not know Neil personally; I knew of him only because I previously attended a gathering held in his tent. Some weeks after my dream, Neil called us out of the blue and said, "The Holy Spirit told me to call you. What are we supposed to do together?"

I was speechless. We didn't even know each other, and there is no way he could have known about my dream. Clearly God was moving again. I told him the dream.

Some may call it a coincidence, but I knew God was up to something. Neil agreed to bring his massive tent to Virginia for a weekend based on this dream. God formed a connection that we never could have contrived.

We found ourselves doing something we never thought we would do. We were in a field in a massive circus tent with thousands of young people, and we were all worshipping our guts out. Worship leaders, artists, ministers, and people from across the nation came together under that huge tent, and there was an expectation in the air that God was going to do something remarkable.

"Everyone pray!" someone shouted as the report of tornadoes came to our attention. And pray we did. A group of young people prayed under the tent for the storm to move around us since we had been praying for months for those attending and we didn't want to miss what God had for us. As they were praying, someone yelled for everyone to come out and see what was happening. To our shock there was a beautiful opening of clear sky in the clouds above us.

I saw this as a kiss from God, an acknowledgment not only that He loved the sound of our prayers and worship but also that He could stop a storm if that's what it took to accomplish His purposes. I had no idea at the time that this was only a precursor of the miraculous feats He was about to perform. We continued in prayer at the furnace, unaware that something was coming that none of us was expecting.

A Surprising Prophecy

As if once weren't enough, we set the circus tent up a second time for our annual Awaken the Dawn gathering in 2011. This time Bob Jones came. Bob was a respected prophetic minister. He was in his eighties at the time yet had an extremely busy schedule, and we were thrilled and honored that he would join us in our tent gathering.

Before the main event later that day, Bob joined our leadership team in a small tent beside the larger one to talk, pray, and listen for what God might be saying. As we gathered in prayer, a small smile washed over Bob's face and he said with his Arkansas drawl, "I've got something for you."

What he shared with us that day has become widely repeated in our world. He said, "You are going to be a part of tent gatherings. The youth of America are going to gather. It'll be like a Holy Spirit Woodstock or a new Jesus movement. There will be portable toilets and hot dog stands beyond your wildest imagination."

Portable toilets and hot dog stands beyond our wildest imagination? What on earth was this man talking about? It definitely got my attention, because almost as soon as he finished speaking, many of us found ourselves suddenly on our faces. This time we weren't in a little prayer room or on a nice red-carpeted church floor—we were in the dirt in a field under a tent.

A Big Vision

I knew God had spoken powerfully through Bob Jones, but even months later I had no idea what the Lord was actually telling us. Then a couple of months after Bob Jones spoke to us, a friend of mine in our prayer community had a dream. In this guy's dream he walked up to me and some others and said there was going to be a gathering on the East Coast of America, and twelve groups were going to join together in a combined effort. I told him in the dream that it was impossible. Then a voice came from behind us and said, "With man it is impossible, but I will do it." It was God speaking in the dream.

After the man shared that dream with me, I was troubled and excited. This seemed to resonate with what Bob Jones had said to us but also seemed like an intimidating prospect. I knew a gathering like this would take God's intervention and supernatural help.

I decided to talk to some friends, namely Lou Engle, who has been a spiritual father to me and has organized countless gatherings all over the nation, including TheCall; and Andy Byrd, who is brilliantly leading The Send in stadiums worldwide. Both men were out West, so I booked a flight to Orange County, California, where I had arranged to talk with Andy, Lou, and another friend named Brian Brennt, cofounder of a student/young adult–focused movement called the Circuit Riders.

Right after I booked my flight, I got a phone call from a leader in Kansas City, Missouri, who had no idea about my plan to meet with Andy, Lou, and Brian. He said he had a dream the night before in which I was meeting with Andy Byrd. I told him I just booked a flight to meet with Andy the day before! Then he said something that completely shocked me. He said there would be a gathering on the East Coast with twelve groups coming together. It was almost the same sentence my friend had heard in his dream!

As powerful and gripping as these dreams and encounters were, I was still unclear on what God wanted me to do. So I asked my wife, Ashley, "What if we go on a one-week fast together to see if God will tell us anything about what this means?" She agreed.

We didn't tell anybody about the fast. I was asking God to confirm this wild idea of gathering on the East Coast. Specifically I wanted to know if God wanted us to gather on the National Mall in Washington, DC, to do on a national level what we had been doing in our little prayer room in Virginia and at our national gatherings. In my conversations with Lou Engle and many others, the idea of this gathering being on the National Mall had come up multiple times. Then my wife reminded me of some dreams she had about our gathering on the National Mall, and Jesus walking in our midst. They were powerful dreams. I was gripped.

Was I supposed to call all of America to the National Mall? This seemed so lofty. I knew I was going on a journey with Jesus to hear His voice and obey Him. I was also still trying to figure out how Bob Jones' word about the tents and the portable johns applied to any of this. I wanted to say yes to whatever God asked me to do, but I was also counting the cost, and I wanted to be sure I was hearing correctly. I didn't want to jump into anything this big without it clearly being from God. I asked Him to speak some more.

A couple of days into our fast, I received a message from an old friend. He said he just had a dream in which he walked up to me in a large crowd of people at a gathering that I was helping lead and said, "The Holy Spirit says to not be afraid to do the new thing He has told you to do." What? I hadn't mentioned this to anyone but my wife. There was no way he could have known that was the exact question I was asking the Lord. This had to be a confirmation.

After our fast I had to travel to an event in Atlanta that Lou Engle also was participating in. I told Lou about my friend's dream and asked him if God was leading him to lead an event on the National Mall, because if he was, we would join him.

Lou told me at that time, "You're the one with the story line. If you pull the trigger, we'll go with *you*." This shook me.

I was still not convinced we were the ones to pull the trigger, but I took what Lou was saying seriously.

"What's the next step?" I asked Lou, still reeling from his counsel to pull the trigger on a large-scale national gathering.

"You should talk to Chris," Lou said. Chris is one of Lou's most trusted friends who often prays with Lou to receive direction and discern what God is saying to him. I was in Atlanta having this conversation with Lou, and Chris lived in Kansas City, Missouri, and knew nothing about it.

About thirty minutes after this conversation with Lou Engle, I headed to the airport to fly home. While in line to board my flight to Virginia, I looked up, and standing in front of me was Chris!

This is the exact person Lou had just said I should talk to next to determine what God was saying I should do. I knew immediately this meeting was impossible unless God was involved. Chris did not even know I was in Atlanta, much less on the same flight. Lou didn't know he was there either. I didn't tell Chris much, but on that flight, Chris said he felt strongly that the Holy Spirit was showing him 2017 was the year for this gathering. Unbelievable!

You would think after all this I would be pretty convinced. But a bit like Gideon in the Bible, I still wanted more confirmation. Two months after my meeting with Chris, Heidi Baker came to speak at a gathering we hosted in Virginia Beach, and I shared with her this whole story about going to the Mall and got pretty raw with her about my struggle. How on earth was I supposed to pull the trigger, to use Lou's language, on something involving the whole nation when most of my ministry experience was leading a little prayer room hidden away in Virginia?

"I'm still not sure what I'm supposed to do," I said.

"Well, I know exactly what you're supposed to do," she replied. "But maybe God will say something to you tonight."

Well, God did speak something to me that night—through Heidi. Right there on stage, in front of thousands of people, she called me out. "David Bradshaw, if God says to go to the National Mall, you go to the National Mall. You're allowed to ask how, but you cannot say no."

I had never been publicly rebuked before—especially by a legendary missionary like Heidi Baker. But there was so much tenderness in her words. They moved me. It was like the Father was tenderly rebuking me through this mother, and something clicked. It was now clear to me that it was time to step out of the boat.

Getting Out of the Boat

Jason Hershey is one of my heroes. At the time of this writing, he has been hosting 24/7 worship in a tent on the National Mall for over five years. This ongoing worship on the Mall is called David's Tent DC. Since Jason was already in DC praying and had authority in that space, I knew I needed to call him and process this whole story with him.

He had been the one laboring faithfully on the Mall in a way no one had labored before. It was right that he be a part of this. One of the amazing things about Jesus is that He works through friendships. He doesn't want anybody doing ministry alone. He often gives different people different parts of the story, but each part is completely dependent on the others. In this case my conversation with Jason Hershey made things so much clearer.

God clearly said to go to the National Mall; I now knew that. And Bob Jones gave me a word about tent cities and the youth of America. Then Jason called me one day and said, "It's not one tent; it's fifty tents, one for every state." It was like a bomb went off in my heart. Who had ever dreamed up such a concept? How would we fill fifty tents 24/7? This would require thousands of musicians coming to DC on their own dime. To my knowledge nothing like this had ever been attempted.

"Either this is God," I said, "or we are crazy." When I hung up the phone, I told my wife about the conversation with Jason. She felt the same way I did—we *had* to do this.

So Jason and I and a couple of others went to the National Park Service to reserve almost the entire National Mall for a three-day event. Let me tell you, that was another crazy day in my life. In a surprising divine twist, we accidentally booked the National Mall during the Feast of Tabernacles. That is the biblical Jewish holiday when the Israelites would set up tents in Jerusalem and people would come to their nation's capital to thank God for His blessings. We were reserving our nation's capital to set up tents at that same time.

To add to the drama, the load-in day on our permit to begin setting up for the National Mall event was October 4. We found out that October 4, 2017, was the twenty-year anniversary of what was arguably one of the largest gatherings on the National Mall. By some estimates Promise Keepers' Stand in the Gap event brought together nearly one million men in prayer and repentance in 1997. When we realized the significance of that date, my friends and I just stood there with our jaws dropped in astonishment. Could it get any crazier?

Lou kept his promise and went with us to the National Mall, but it turned out to be a whirlwind in his world as well. On the last of our four days on the Mall, Lou and his team hosted a phenomenal gathering of tens of thousands of women called Rise Up.

We found language for what we believed God wanted to do through our event on the Mall in the psalms. Although Psalm 68 is really about Jesus' return and His procession into Jerusalem, it also speaks about David bringing the ark, which represents God's presence, into Jerusalem. When the psalm was written, David described the return of the ark as "the procession of my God and King into the sanctuary" (v. 24).

In Psalm 68 we found an expression of the dream God placed in our hearts way back in those first few days of 24/7 prayer at our church community in Fredericksburg. Now we were issuing an invitation to America to gather not around speakers or personalities but around the presence of God.

Psalm 68 talks about singers and musicians going before the ark. As wild as it sounded, God dropped the dream in our hearts of inviting thousands of musicians to fill what turned out to be fifty-eight tents and sing love songs to Jesus 24/7 in our nation's capital. This was not just an event. It was an offering of love from thousands of people from every state—even more than the twelve groups Bob Jones prophesied.

I walked the National Mall the day before the crowds showed up. I was looking at tents from one end of the Mall to the other. I ran into someone who worked at the Smithsonian museums. He asked me what was going on. He said he had never seen so many tents on the Mall in all his sixteen years of working in Washington, DC. He asked exactly the right question: "Why?" Why would anyone set up fifty-eight tents at the center of DC and sing around the clock? There's more than one answer to that, some of which we've already discussed. But at the end of the day there is one answer, and it was the driving force behind all of this: Jesus is worthy of being worshipped in the center of the nation's most powerful city.

In Mark 14 there was a woman who poured very costly perfume on Jesus while He was sitting in a crowded room. That perfume was worth about a year's wages at the time. Some who were present thought her offering was a complete waste and said so aloud. But right then and there Jesus validated her. He said, "Leave her alone....She has done a beautiful thing to me" (v. 6). Jesus' ways seem backward to the world. But the world needs more than human ingenuity. Our human efforts are not enough. We need the presence of God at the center of our cities and nations to bring transformation that is beyond human explanation.

This is what I believed God was up to. He was inviting thousands of musicians and lovers of God to fill the city that represents the epicenter of political power to present an offering of love to Jesus, the likes of which Washington had never seen.

THE TENT CITY

About fifty thousand people showed up on the National Mall in October 2017, and sixteen hundred worship and prayer groups from all fifty states led shifts in the tents. Hundreds of thousands viewed it online. It was called Awaken the Dawn 2017.

To our amazement, people threw their instruments onto airplanes or put them in their cars and drove across the nation on their own dime to give Jesus an offering of love. Some drove across the country just to take a middle-of-the-night set on an unplugged sound system because we couldn't have the sound on overnight on the Mall. One couple sold their house and bought a bus, which they now live in as they travel the country sharing Jesus.

During those four days, it was as if heaven came down in Washington, DC. Many people were saved. Many people were healed. Deaf ears opened. The city was looking on, asking what in the world was happening. Every single tent was a prophecy that Jesus is alive and He is worth everything.

The tents on the Mall were like little windows into each state. You could walk down the Mall and worship with Georgia or California without having to jump on an airplane! Every tent represented a region of our nation, and everyone got to be a part. The body of Christ in America was unified for one reason alone—to worship the One who is worthy. There was power in that oneness. When the body of Christ comes together, the atmosphere shifts. Worship, not politics or personality, had drawn these people to our nation's capital.

Amazingly during and after the event we received remarkable reports, including of top government officials getting saved and washing one another's feet across party lines—all while the worship was going on around-the-clock.

One of the park police told us there was a buzz among law enforcement patrolling the National Mall because there was very little crime at a time when there was typically much more criminal activity. Some of these police attributed it to the worship on the Mall.

I had some of the most amazing times while walking the

Mall in the middle of the night during those four days. I might not have believed it was possible if I hadn't been there. Fifty-eight tents were filled with people worshipping their hearts out. Fifty-eight tents filled the atmosphere with songs of love for our Savior. What once felt like an unlikely dream actually happened, and it spawned incredible testimonies.

SHAME REMOVED

Because Jesus' eyes are not just on nations but on individuals, let me tell you one person's story from those four days. I will call her Anna. I met her a couple of weeks after the gathering in DC. She and her family came to me crying as they told the story. While on the Mall, Anna had her eyes closed and was worshipping Jesus with all her heart.

Someone on the main stage in the middle of all the tents said God was going to remove scars on people's bodies from self-harm. Anna had scars all over her arms and legs from cutting, having suffered from self-hatred for years. No one prayed for Anna directly. She was just pouring out her heart in love for Jesus. Then all of a sudden she felt hands on her back. But there was no one there that she could see.

Shortly afterward she saw that every single scar on her body caused by self-harm was gone. That day Jesus removed her shame. That's one story among many. But it really happened, and these kinds of things will continue to happen as we go public with worship and gospel proclamation in our cities and campuses.

THE BIRTH OF A MOVEMENT

One of the greatest things that happened during those four days on the National Mall was that a family and a movement were born. My friends from California brought thirty worship teams to fill the California tent. By the time they returned to

California, they were family, though many had not known each other before then. They started having video calls connecting hundreds of worship leaders from across California who began to dream together for their state and beyond. On the Mall we gathered America around the invisible God, and we discovered Him in one another.

After the event one of our leaders reminded us of a vision she had years earlier. In the vision Jesus was standing in Washington, DC, surrounded by people. Suddenly Jesus began to walk across a map of the United States, and all the people who were with Him in DC began to move together. Every time they arrived at a state capital, a group from that state would break off and gather in their capital, and she saw the Holy Spirit fall in each state.

In 2018, the year after our gathering on the National Mall, we invited Christians in all fifty states to gather prayer groups from throughout their states for fifty hours of worship, prayer, and gospel proclamation in tents in their state capitals. This movement happened simultaneously in every state capital. We called it Tent America. At the same time this was happening, students at just over one hundred universities hosted around-the-clock worship in tents on their campuses. This brought the total to over 150 tents across America filled with prayer, worship, and evangelism all at the same time.

Then in 2019 the vision expanded even further. I thought, "What if the gatherings were hosted by anyone, anywhere, not just in the state capitals? How far could this go?" So during the Feast of Tabernacles in 2019, over four hundred cities and campuses signed up to host tent gatherings marked by worship, prayer, and gospel proclamation.

It had become a movement.

But just as importantly it is also a family. My friends Pia Jo Reynolds and Matthew Lilley have helped to coordinate the Awaken the Dawn: National Leadership Network. This is a decentralized network. We are not asking anyone to leave their churches or other ministry organizations. We want to see regions and states connect around the shared value of hosting Jesus' presence and proclaiming the gospel because we are seeing a family of believers emerge from these efforts, and that family continues to grow.

We are continuing to see churches and praying groups form relationships in their own regions and across the nation even to this day. They are working together as one body yet still operating in their own local churches and groups without competition or a need for fame and credit. Their ambition is His fame as they gather and pray. Could this be part of the prayer for unity and love Jesus uttered before He went to the cross? I believe so. God is bringing an interconnectedness of praying and presence-centered communities.

And He is launching a movement of Neverites.

Chapter 5

THE CALL OF THE NEVERITES

Then the man brought me by way of the north gate to the front of the temple. I looked and saw the glory of the LORD filling the temple of the LORD, and I fell facedown.

—EZEKIEL 44:4

WHY WOULD GOD start a national movement of prayer and worship flowing out of tents? Something happened nearly two years before the 2017 gathering on the National Mall that may help us understand.

It was December 2014, and I got an urgent call from a long-time friend named Brian Hume. He asked if we could meet on a specific day. I agreed. Brian has a long track record of hearing from God for others, so my interest was piqued. Even though I've known Brian for years, it still surprised me when he walked into my office and threw $444 on my desk in small denominations so it looked like an even larger amount of money.

"I have a word for you," he said.

Sometimes when God speaks, He uses parables—word pictures and stories. I believe He does this because He wants to make it both hard and easy to understand what He's saying. Parabolic language requires you to reach for the meaning. Jesus taught in parables during His three-year ministry in Israel for this reason. Only those hungry to hear God usually understand what He is saying when He speaks in parables.

But parables also can make understanding easier because the story and symbolism help us remember what He is saying. The parable actually can make the concept more accessible to those who are hungry to hear. Brian's message to me was one of those parabolic words.

I was more than a decade into leading day-and-night prayer, just trying to keep my head down and stay connected to Jesus and what He asked me to do. Then Brian walks in my office, slaps a huge pile of cash on my desk, and tells me something that would prove to be life-changing.

"The Holy Spirit says that you are in a 444-day transition, and on the other side of this 444 days you will have clarity about the next season," he said. "God is also going to speak to you from biblical passages that have the reference 444."

I had no idea what Brian was talking about, but I was grateful for the 444 dollars. "Well, Brian, we'll have to wait and see what all this is about," I said.

Just weeks later one of our leaders at the Prayer Furnace who works primarily with Gen Z (those born between 1997 and 2015) came to me and said the previous night he had a dream. In it there was a crowd of Gen Z students. He saw me there, and worship was exploding among these students. Then he looked at his watch in the dream, and he saw that it was exactly 4:44. Then he woke up.

As he was lying in bed, the presence of God became overwhelmingly strong in his room—so strong in fact that he started asking God for mercy. What caught my attention from this young leader's experience was that the time was 4:44, and the room was full of students. His dream had the number Brian had given me: 444.

A few weeks later a friend of mine shared yet another dream. In it I was preaching on Ezekiel 44:4:

> Then the man brought me by way of the north gate
> to the front of the temple. I looked and saw the glory
> of the LORD filling the temple of the LORD, and I fell
> facedown.

This is the passage in which God's presence and glory come to fill a new temple. I believe the ecstatic experience Ezekiel had thousands of years ago has a yet future fulfillment, and the fullness will not be realized until Jesus returns. However, the principle of what God has been saying to us and what I have been describing in this book is that God wants His presence to dwell with communities of believers on college campuses and in cities across the US and around the world.

In my friend's dream, as I was preaching on Ezekiel 44:4, another one of our leaders named Sebastian walked up to him and said, "Have you heard the new message that David is preaching? It's about the call of the Neverites."

"You mean Nazirites?" my friend asked in the dream. Nazirite is a term in the Bible for those who give themselves to God in unusual consecration.

"No, it's the call of the Neverites."

Neverites? What a strange word. I suppose God sometimes is in the business of inventing words. This dream was clearly from God, especially in light of Brian's word about biblical passages with the 444 reference.

Upon waking up from this dream, my friend said he felt the Holy Spirit say the Neverites are those who never let the fire on the altar go out, who never stop saying, "Holy, holy, holy." They are those who never leave the presence of God or the tent of meeting.

In Exodus 33:11 we see this posture in Joshua. His gaze was fixed on the Lord. He was so fascinated with God, he refused to leave God's presence, even after Moses left the tent of meeting. This was not really unique to Joshua, however. This was the pattern in the life of Isaiah. This was the pattern in the life of Paul. This was the model in the life of Jesus Himself. This is becoming the pattern of this generation. The people of one thing get everything. Jesus is after the gaze of our hearts and the affections of this generation. We have presented all the ways the gospel can help our lives. We have called people into moral lifestyles and sound doctrine. But the greatest invitation is to know God, possess mesmerized hearts of love and holy fascination, and experience ongoing encounters with Him.

The Neverites are those who have single vision for the one thing David dreamed about three thousand years ago. They have vision for what Jesus prayed in John 17:26—that we would love Him like the Father loves Him—and for Jesus' presence to dwell in their cities and church communities.

Before we went to the National Mall in 2017, when I was still discussing with a number of leaders the prospect of hosting such a crazy gathering, they asked me to write down what God was saying. So I wrote the story I just shared with you about how God was leading us. Sometime after I hit send on the email to the leaders, I realized it was exactly the 444th day since Brian came to my office and told me about this transition of 444 days. I later realized the transition happened in the exact timeline Brian said.

What transpired on the National Mall in October of 2017 was the launching of a movement of Neverites. They are young and old and cannot be defined primarily by a political party or denominational background. They are dreaming an ancient dream and embody the lifestyle of worship, prayer, and gospel proclamation necessary to see transformation all around them. The Neverites are here, and they are yet to come. God is issuing a call to every generation to step into the Neverite calling because when they do, it will change the world.

SMALL IS THE NEW BIG

The word from Brian and the subsequent dreams were so clear. But how was I to carry the calling of the Neverite to a new generation? One of the answers came as I drove through

Pennsylvania to speak at a Youth With A Mission (YWAM) Discipleship Training School.

It was late, and I was on a phone call as I tried to navigate the Pennsylvania roads with my headphones jammed into my ears. This particular call was with hundreds of amazing people who were praying for America. They asked me to share a few words, and I began to tell them about the word Brian had given me and the need to invite the next generation to host the presence of Jesus.

These interceding moms and dads started praying into this prophetic story line. As I was driving through the mountains of Pennsylvania, listening to the prayers going up from coast to coast on this call, I noticed my phone was blowing up with text messages from the leader of our young adult group. "Call me as soon as you get this!" he wrote. It was almost midnight by the time I got off my other call, but I called him immediately.

"What is going on?" I asked.

"You will never believe what just happened."

He was clearly emotional, so I probed further. "What's going on, man?" The suspense had me on the edge of my seat.

He went on to describe what took place among a small group of young adults he was with that night at a meeting in someone's living room. They had a guitar and began to worship as usual. Then something happened. Worship became unstoppable. They all lost track of time. They got lost in God's presence. They began to lose all thought of themselves and could only think about Jesus. Suddenly they all had a vision at the same time, mostly with their eyes open. They all saw it. I pushed him on this point, knowing that sometimes people can exaggerate in a moment of excitement when telling stories.

"Your eyes were open? Everyone saw it?"

"Yes, we all saw it," he said. "And I stood up, sensing God as strongly as I have ever sensed Him, and said that a student awakening is coming. It is really coming."

Then they all saw a light, and it filled the room.

That alone is amazing, but what struck me was that this happened while I was sharing about the calling of the Neverites on the prayer call. Hundreds were praying at that exact moment for the next generation to be awakened to give themselves completely to seeking Jesus. At that exact time, Jesus gave our little community of young people a taste of the reality of His nearness to confirm this very word about the calling of the Neverites.

What's also notable about this is that it happened in a living room, not in a stadium. This movement is not mostly about large gatherings. Small is the new big. This movement is for everyone everywhere. Revival is not the ability to fill a stadium. It is when all eyes are on Jesus and communities of believers are living in love and serving one another. Yes, we will have large-scale events in stadiums. I am personally involved in organizing these kinds of gatherings. But the stadium events are really the overflow of what's happening in living rooms, dorm rooms, local churches, and families that host Jesus' presence and together live out the principles in the Sermon on the Mount. This is key. You can do this wherever you are—that's the genius of it.

I think it's time to give this generation permission to become the wild-eyed lovers of God they were born to be. This, I believe, is right at the core of what God is longing to do. Right now it's becoming increasingly apparent that there is no human remedy for the problems we are facing in America or the nations. But there is a remedy, and He has a name: Jesus.

PART II

HOLY HEARTS

Chapter 6

SURPRISED BY LOVE

She loves. He is love. She is thirsty. He is a fountain.
—Bernard of Clairvaux

O<small>NE NIGHT, AT</small> a critical time in my life, God spoke to me in the most profound way about our ministry. It was early 2017, and the night before, I had made the huge announcement that we were hosting four days of 24/7 prayer and worship at the National Mall in the fall of that year. I shared our plan to set up fifty tents for fifty states and invite thousands of musicians and singers to lead us in around-the-clock worship and prayer. The announcement was broadcast live from a church in Washington, DC, and was viewed not just across the US but around the world.

The paperwork for the permits had been signed, so it was official. We were planning to do something that had never been done—something that came with an incredibly high price tag—and we were committing to do this in front of tens of thousands of people.

In all honesty, after making this announcement, I started to panic.

As I lay in bed that night, I could feel the weight of what we had just committed to. I felt exposed and vulnerable. I had literally signed my name on the dotted line of what God had asked me to do, and now I was at His mercy. It was a test of my faith on a grand scale. I even had some close friends and leaders questioning the plan. Others had sacrificed for this too, and we needed God to come through and provide.

In the middle of the night, after having gone to bed with

these thoughts buzzing in my mind, I was jolted awake. I went from a deep sleep to wide awake with my heart racing in a second.

I heard an audible voice.

It sounded like my natural father's voice, and He said only one word: my name, "David." In one of my most profound moments of insecurity, God spoke identity to my heart by simply calling my name in the middle of the night. That's all He said. That's all I needed to hear.

Ironically I was scheduled to speak the next morning at our church, Awakening Community Church, about the Father's love. I had the whole message prepared. But as I stood up before the church that morning, I broke down in tears. God spoke the one thing I needed to hear more than anything else, and it was not strategy; it was affection.

This is the only time I've heard God speak with my natural ears. Most people I know have never heard God speak audibly. But whether or not you hear His voice out loud, the fact is this: if you are in Christ, the Father loves you as He loves His own Son, Jesus (John 17:23). This defines your identity.

When it comes down to it, we are all in a frenzy to find our identities, and mostly we are looking in all the wrong places and making all the wrong choices. We find our identities in the places we get a sense of self-worth, and the multitude of things that are fueling most people's sense of identity—sexuality, careers, power and position, the list goes on—are falling short. Many people are experiencing an identity crisis at their cores because they just don't feel successful or fulfilled. Jesus answers the crisis. Hosting Jesus' presence is largely about discovering Jesus' personality, and this leads to His shaping our identities.

I'm convinced the encounter I had with the Father that night was not just for me. I believe He was establishing a culture for this movement of worship, prayer, and gospel proclamation in our cities and college campuses. I believe that all our extravagant songs, prayers, and proclamations are meant to pour out from a river that is flowing on the inside of us. That river is flowing because we have discovered that the One seated on the throne in heaven is a Father who is smiling at each of us individually and personally. Knowing this will wash away all our shame. This revelation is the answer to our identity crisis.

LOVED LIKE JESUS

I believe answers to the most existential questions of life are found in a statement from Jesus in John 17. It is particularly important because it is one of the few places in the Scriptures where we see God talking to God about us. Jesus is praying to the Father right before going to the cross, and you and I are the topic of the conversation. Jesus says in John 17:23, "I in them and you in me—so that they may be brought to complete unity. Then the world will know that you sent me and have loved them even as you have loved me."

Jesus says that God the Father loves us in the same way and to the same degree that He loves Jesus. There is literally nothing more powerful than the love God has for God, which is the love the Father has for Jesus. If it were not in red letters, it would be impossible to believe God feels the same way about us as He does about Jesus. But it is true, and it is the defining reality of our lives.

John said that we love God "because he first loved us" (1 John 4:19). As we are pursuing Jesus, every one of us has the urgent need in the depths of our beings to know that we are enjoyed by God, even in our weaknesses and despite our failures. We need a regular reintroduction to the goodness of God. The struggle to believe this is one of the most important battles you'll face in your life, no matter how long you have been a follower of Jesus.

We are trying to love Him, but God flips the script and says,

"This is not so much about your learning to love Me but about your learning to first receive My love for you."

When we look up at God, it is not His power and sovereignty that shock us most profoundly. The greatest surprise and wonder of God is that we look up and see that He has a smile on His face as He looks at us.

In the midst of His fearful, glorious presence, there is a smiling Father.

Our natural thinking does not expect or embrace God's affections on this level. We naturally reject it. We expect to hear a rebuke as the main topic of conversation when we are approaching God. However, if you are hearing only rebukes in your heart after you've turned to Jesus, you are not hearing accurately yet.

Even as a natural father, I know I need to communicate my affection to my children more than my rebukes. God is pursuing us more than we are pursuing Him. As Hans Urs Von Balthasar wrote in his profound book *Prayer*, "The better a man learns to pray, the more deeply he finds that all his stammering is only an answer to God's speaking to him."[1]

There is no way to grow outside of this revelation of how God feels about you. As you read this, you may find it unbelievable because you know your own failures. Repentance is absolutely required, but repentance is not pulling yourself up by the bootstraps and fixing yourself. It is turning from the sin that is bringing nothing but death and giving yourself to Jesus alone. It is total and complete surrender.

This is the core truth: God likes you, and He passionately desires you, even in your weakness. Today is the day to return home like that prodigal who finally came to his senses. When that son in Luke 15 who had squandered his father's money and lived a reckless life finally decided to return to the father's house, do you know how the father responded?

Jesus said that while his son was still a long way off, the

father saw him, ran to him, and kissed him. He ran. This is a picture of our loving God—He is the God who runs to you.

The Dutch theologian Henri Nouwen wrote:

> For most of my life I struggled to find God, to know God, to love God. I have tried hard to follow the guidelines of the spiritual life—pray always, work for others, read the Scriptures—and to avoid the many temptations to dissipate myself. I have failed many times but always tried again, even when I was close to despair.
>
> Now I wonder whether I have sufficiently realized during all this time God has been trying to find me, to know me, and to love me....The question is not "How am I to love God?" but "How am I to let myself be loved by God?" God is looking into the distance for me, trying to find me, and longing to bring me home.[2]

Let me flesh this out theologically. God has all power (omnipotence) and all knowledge (omniscience), but His core nature is love. Even before He created humans, He was love. He has been defined as love for billions of years, and the love of God is what flowed among the Father, Son, and Holy Spirit. God has always been love; therefore, He must be a plurality—three persons and yet one. God didn't become a loving Father after He created us; He has always been a Father with a family within His being. We were actually created to be participants in this love flowing within God's person, and it is intensely personal. You are breathing because God wants to share Himself.

David didn't get to the place of the "one thing" in his life just because he had a uniquely passionate or focused personality. He got there in his heart because he experienced God's absolute goodness. He said, "Your gentleness makes me great" (Ps. 18:35, NASB).

After Moses asked to see God's glory in Exodus 33:18, God said He would cause all His goodness to pass before him (Exod.

33:19). That is because the glory of God is the goodness of God. It was not His power that He made pass before Moses but His goodness.

The reality is that we are dealing with a generation of people who are wrestling with an orphan mindset, perhaps more than any previous generation has, at least in America. When you have an orphan mindset, you invariably hurt other people because you are trying to protect yourself. God wants to heal your heart so you can actually love others without self-preservation. That is why the Holy Spirit is called the Spirit of adoption:

> For you did not receive the spirit of slavery to fall back into fear, but you have received the Spirit of adoption as sons, by whom we cry, "Abba! Father!"
> —ROMANS 8:15, ESV

The result of this revelation of the measure of God's love for us is something that is eluding many of us: rest for your restless heart. There is no more need for competition or anxiety, because you have already arrived in God's house. Perhaps you picked up this book to read the story of a movement of worship, prayer, and gospel proclamation, and here I am talking about Jesus as love incarnate. That is where we must start to experience the life-altering presence we are called to host. Understanding and sharing the Father's love is the greatest adventure of all.

Becoming Love

The end of Jesus' prayer in John 17 is just as important as the passage we discussed previously. In His final words before going to the cross, Jesus said this:

> I made known to them [all who believe in Jesus] your name, and I will continue to make it known, that the

love with which you have loved me may be in them,
and I in them.

—JOHN 17:26, ESV

This statement from Jesus provides the apologetic for the movement described in this book. What is the Holy Spirit doing? He is doing a lot of things, but I can tell you beyond the shadow of a doubt the main thing He is doing: He is answering this prayer of Jesus' when He asked God to cause us to love Him as the Father loves Him.

I really want you to catch the magnitude of this. Jesus asked the Father to cause us to love Him *like the Father loves Him.* How does God feel about God? How does the Father feel about Jesus? There is no end to that shoreless ocean. We are invited into this kind of love. It's no wonder God intends to fill the earth with singing.

One of my spiritual fathers, Mike Bickle, said that after he started the International House of Prayer in Kansas City, Missouri, which has hosted 24/7 worship and prayer for over twenty years now, many people approached him and congratulated him for a dream fulfilled. His reply was that the house of prayer was his assignment. His dream is what happens in his heart when God reveals Himself to him—when he grows in the greatest commandment, which is to love God with all your heart, mind, soul, and strength. He said he has found that he loves God more now than he did years ago.

I believe him, and I, like the biblical David, want to make loving God more and more my greatest goal in life. This is both the launching pad and the endgame of all prayer, revival, and missions.

THE CROSS HAS SPOKEN

You may be wondering, How can God love us so much in the midst of our brokenness and in light of our sin and failure?

First, it is His character to love. He is more merciful than any of us. Having said that, there is one profound reason we can have this relationship of love and enjoyment: the cross of Christ.

On the cross Jesus not only died in our place; He took our shame, punishment, sin, and brokenness. He took it all. It is finished. All who have surrendered their lives to Jesus and trust in Him are as holy as Jesus is because of what He accomplished at Calvary.

We don't have to be good enough to receive God's love—we can't be. The cross silences human pride. It is the ultimate expression of love and justice. Because of Jesus' death and resurrection, you and I are now in the family of God as His children forever. God had the final word in Jesus' work on the cross.

The Kiss of the Word

There is one practical key that is perhaps the most important of all to receiving the love of Christ. It is expressed in the Song of Solomon.

The Song of Solomon, or the Song of Songs in some Bible translations, is an eight-chapter love song written by David's son Solomon. Many people skip this poetic book because of all its pomegranates and palm trees. But at its core it is a picture of love between a man and his wife. Marriage is probably the greatest analogy Scripture gives to show us what God's relationship with His people looks like. Paul said marriage speaks of Christ and the church (Eph. 5:32). This is why seeing Jesus as the eternal Bridegroom helps us better understand God's love for us.

In the first chapter of the Song of Solomon, the bride says, "Let him kiss me with the *kisses of his mouth*! For your love is better than wine" (v. 2, ESV, emphasis added). The Song of Solomon is an allegory of Christ's relationship with the church, and it's important to understand that this verse is not in any way referring to a physical relationship with Jesus. It is analogous to the Word of God touching our hearts when it is communicated by the Holy Spirit.

The Word is a kiss from God on your heart. Allowing the Holy Spirit to touch your heart with the Word of God is the greatest tool for growing in love. That's when you discover that Jesus' love is "better than wine." Wine speaks of the pleasures of the world, not all of which are sinful. God's love communicated to your heart is better than any pleasure the world could offer us. It is the highest form of pleasure. That is why David, the great theologian of joy, said, "In your presence there is fullness of joy; at your right hand there are pleasures forevermore" (Ps. 16:11, ESV).

How do we receive God's kiss on our hearts? This happens when we take the time to meditate on the Bible and use the Word to engage in a conversation with Jesus. This is called praying the Bible, and this is how it works.

Find key verses that speak of God's heart and what He has done through Jesus. Study them so that you don't miss the context. But just as importantly, turn them into a conversation with God directly. Ask God questions about the verse. Pray each phrase back to Him. Use your own language to express what the verse is saying back to God in a dialogue. You may even want to sing it. Commit out loud to obey anything the text says to do. Write in a journal what God is revealing to your heart from the passage. Do this regularly. The Holy Spirit thrives in communicating God's affections to you, and if you pray His Word, He will reveal Himself more and more to you over time.

Teresa of Ávila was a great contemplative from the sixteenth century known for spending copious amounts of time in prayer. The more time she spent with God, the more deeply she came to love Him. She once described her prayer time this way:

The consolation, the sweetness, and the delight are incomparably greater than that experienced [previously]....This prayer is a glorious foolishness, a heavenly madness....Often I had been as though bewildered and inebriated in this love....The soul would desire to cry out praises, and it is beside itself....It cannot bear so much joy....It would want to be all tongues so as to praise the Lord.[3]

Much of our prayer lives is not like what Teresa describes, and that is not a sign that we lack love for Jesus. Seemingly small encounters with God really matter; they are real and they do change us. I share this quote to provoke you and me to begin to seek God's kiss on our hearts and raise our expectations of what is available.

The greatest supernatural event that is taking place is not tents that host God's presence being set up around the world; it is that broken people are discovering who God is and are beginning to love God the way God loves God.

It's like the Moravians of old used to say, "May the Lamb receive the reward of his suffering."[4] What is that reward? It's not simply our mandatory obedience. It is realized when Jesus captures our hearts and affections above everything else and then we live in affection-based, complete obedience to Him.

Jesus, You have won us over. We are freely Yours forever.

Chapter 7

THERE IS NO RISK
(THOUGH THERE SURE SEEMS TO BE)

During the last three years and three months, I never have asked anyone for anything. The Lord has graciously supplied all my needs as I bring them to Him. At the close of each of these four years, although my income has been comparatively great, I have had only a few shillings left. My needs are met each day by the help of God.
—GEORGE MÜLLER, *THE AUTOBIOGRAPHY OF GEORGE MÜLLER*

"I THINK YOU PICKED the wrong person."

Those were my words to the Lord in the months leading up to the National Mall gathering in 2017. I was beginning to feel the weight of my yes to God as the enormity of the undertaking set in—hosting an event on the National Mall, especially one that spanned several days, costs millions of dollars that I neither had nor knew how we would get. Tens of thousands of people were expected to attend, with more watching via livestream all over the world, and we were going to need fifty-eight tents, nine large sound systems, and countless generators, all of which required funding. Plus we learned that when organizing an event in DC, you have to pay for extra police, EMS, and much more. This was a shock to me. I even questioned whether the event was a wise way to spend money. I want to serve people who are in need, so I wondered if we should spend such a large amount of money on a gathering for worship and gospel proclamation.

But Jesus seemed to be insisting that we proceed. I didn't know how everything was going to work out, but what I did know was that God said to host this gathering. I was certain of that. There are only a few times in my life about which I can say without a doubt that I received a "thus says the Lord" word from God, and this was one of them. I was compelled to keep going because I felt that if I didn't step out and do this, I would stand before Jesus one day and regret my decision. I never want it to be said that Jesus clearly asked me to do something and I did not do that very thing, no matter how outlandish it may have seemed.

That doesn't mean I didn't think God should have picked someone else, someone who had more resources. We were still in significant financial need even the night before the event, and this became a great pain point in my heart. If I had known then what I know now, then I wouldn't have worried about anything. But at the time I was still learning that sometimes God deliberately waits until just the right moment to answer our prayers—that is, His right moment, not ours.

Swallowing a Nail

A few months before the gathering in Washington, I had taken my wife and kids on a short family getaway into DC, and our plan was to then return home. But as we were about to leave, my wife and I both felt strongly that I needed to stay in DC to walk and pray. I was feeling both excitement and trepidation about what was coming, and I needed some time alone to clear my head. My wife planned to drive back home with the kids. Even though I didn't have a vehicle with me, the sense we had was strong enough that we decided I should stay in the city. I would figure out my ride home later. Sometimes you just follow where the Holy Spirit is leading, even if it doesn't make sense.

Alone in DC, I began to walk the Mall and pray. As I looked up and down the long green space, I tried to envision something that still seemed like a pipe dream—scores of tents and thousands of musicians filling the area.

It was a hot summer day, and I was wearing a T-shirt and jeans. I did not expect to connect with anyone that day and was not prepared for any meetings. But while I was walking, I got a text message from a friend. "I have someone who wants to have a phone call with you. This is someone who is well-known and influential. I want you to tell him the whole story, even the Bob Jones parts. But do it in ten minutes on the phone."

I agreed and took the call.

I found myself on the phone with a well-known man I had seen only on TV. Even though my head was spinning a bit over who I was talking with, I shared as much of the story as I could in ten minutes.

"Where are you?" the man asked.

"I am walking on the National Mall in DC," I said.

"Well, I'm actually in DC for a meeting right now too," he said. "I have some time right now. Can you come over so we can talk some more?" He was just a few blocks from where I was standing at that exact moment.

Stunned and a bit perplexed at what was suddenly happening, I quickly answered, "Of course! I'm on my way."

I walked over in my T-shirt and jeans, trying to figure out how to dress it up at least a little bit so I could be taken seriously. I had nothing but my backpack and Bible, nothing by way of business attire. Fortunately I managed to find a long-sleeved shirt stuffed in my backpack that I could throw on.

This man did not live in DC. He just happened to be visiting the city from across the country. My friend who set up the phone call didn't know I was only a couple of blocks from where the man wanted to meet. We hadn't planned any of it. This was beginning to feel like a divine appointment.

I walked into the room, not knowing at all what to expect. We talked a bit more, and I shared more of the story of what God was doing. He said, "I will wire $100K over to you today." I just about fell out of my chair. Since I already looked a bit disheveled from my walk, I decided to stay cool and pull myself together. This was an answer to prayer! I was so grateful and amazed by God and this man's extreme generosity. The reality was that there was still significant funding to raise, but this was an incredible start. At that point, I knew this definitely was a divine appointment.

Then that night I had a dream. In the dream I was in Lou Engle's house. I saw his son. It wasn't a specific son, just someone I knew in the dream was Lou's son. Suddenly, to my great alarm, his son swallowed a nail. Then the son was me. I was the son who swallowed the nail. I woke up in actual pain.

The next morning, I saw Lou in DC. "I had a horrible dream last night," I said. After I shared it with him, Lou said, "That dream was from God. It is the cross that I have had to bear in taking on national initiatives at great cost in obedience to Jesus." This hit me deeply. Despite the incredible financial gift I had received, the road ahead wasn't going to be an easy one.

There Is No Risk

During this season, I asked Heidi Baker, "How do you take such risks of faith all the time and hold your heart at peace?"

Heidi and her husband, Rolland, feed thousands of people every day in Mozambique through their ministry, Iris Global. They have even seen food multiplied. Heidi and Rolland went to Mozambique in 1995 with no money and nowhere to stay because God told them to go, and God provided. They have since started thousands of churches and witnessed amazing miracles. I knew she had taken many steps of faith that looked like nothing other than risk, so she seemed the right person to ask that question.

Her response was remarkable. "There is no risk when you know God has said to do something," she said. "If I spent significant amounts of time worrying about money and resources,

I never would have had the ability to do what God has asked me to do."

No risk. Well, this journey felt like quite a risk, but I would learn it was part of God's great undoing of me. The message I had preached about having poverty of spirit was being tested. I had taught that those who are poor in spirit no longer possess even their own lives. They belong fully to God. They don't own their ministries, their reputations—everything belongs to Jesus. Is that how I lived? Is that what I truly believed? I had to ask myself, Was Jesus enough for me?

I have a friend named Wayne who is an attorney. He was at a gathering we hosted with Lou Engle, and until then he had never heard anyone talk about prayer and fasting the way Lou does. At the end of the event, he felt the Holy Spirit tell him to go and put his hand on Lou's shoulder. He obeyed, and something happened to him. He couldn't stop feeling called to fast.

He started doing multiple forty-day fasts every year. He was praying and fasting so much, he couldn't put as much time into his law firm as he normally needed to. It was like he was walking with a limp. But he was compelled. He was so hungry for God. Well, wouldn't you know it, his business revenue increased by three times during the season of fasting, even though he devoted fewer hours than ever to his business!

Wayne became a prayer partner in my journey. He told me that one night he was out in his car in the middle of the night weeping in prayer for me. That night he cried, "God, You said to do this. Where is the provision?" The next morning he got a text message from a friend. His friend said he had a dream that night before. He said, "Wayne, you were in your car weeping and praying for something, and God said to call you and tell you the answer is yes. He is going to do what you asked Him for last night." This was all true. Wayne was in his car that night praying.

Wayne had asked for the financial provision for the event

God asked us to lead. And the word Wayne received was encouraging, but the rest of the finances had still not come in. God really does help us as we are weak and yet seek to obey Him. God also seems to enjoy last-minute provision. It keeps us connected to Him.

THE DAY BEFORE

The day before the gathering, we were still about $1.4 million in the red. I share this number so you can feel the weight of the story. Let me repeat: we owed $1.4 million to run an event that was starting the next day. I had signed the permits and vendor contracts. They could come for my house! But we knew God said to host this gathering!

My wife and I were praying in our hotel room in DC. I was broken. When I walked the Mall and looked at all the tents and sound systems, all I could see in my flesh was dollar signs. I felt like I had swallowed a nail. I needed God to show up.

Well, Heidi Baker showed up at the hotel, and I asked her to come to the room where we were praying. As soon as she walked in the room, she had the word of the Lord for us: "There will be enough, and there will be some left over for your provision after this is done." In that moment, lying on the floor of that hotel room, I had one of the most intimate encounters with Jesus I have ever had. Jesus had walked into the room, and I was completely undone. Unbelievable strength came into my heart. I knew this was God strengthening me to do what He called me to do.

By God's grace, and only by God's grace, I was able to leave that hotel room and declare to millions of people on the Mall and viewing online that Jesus is worthy of an unprecedented expression of worship in our nation's capital. Boldness came, and I knew God was moving. He deserves all the glory for everything that happened that day.

As I said, God seems to like waiting until the last minute. After the event we were still about one million dollars in the red. Yes, you read that correctly—we needed *one million dollars*.

What happened next blew my mind. The man I met in that divine appointment in DC a few months earlier paid the rest of our bill. One million dollars. It was a miracle. I had never been part of anything where one person gave so much. I want to honor this man. He had just surrendered his life to Jesus months earlier and gave that offering in obedience to God, not just because there was a need. It was an offering to the Lord, and it was a great sacrifice.

He actually gave a little above the need so there would be some left. I remembered Heidi's word to me in the hotel, and I was shocked.

God knit my heart with this man. The mystery of all of this is that God knits hearts together in love. I began earnestly praying for this man and his destiny. I know it might sound disingenuous, but I love him deeply. I don't feel that way just because he gave so extravagantly. God knit my heart to his. This is actually God's priority in many ways. Love begins to grow in the journey of faith and provision.

Generosity is the culture of heaven. God is generous. He gave everything. He gave His very life. Radical generosity is part of God's nature. And it is true—you cannot outgive God.

Worry Isn't God's Way

As I mentioned, if I could do everything over again, I would do it with no anxiety—just unlimited trust, even if I don't see the way forward with absolute clarity. Worry is never God's way. The Scriptures are clear on this:

> Be anxious for nothing, but in everything by prayer and supplication, with thanksgiving, let your requests be made known to God; and the peace of God, which

> surpasses all understanding, will guard your hearts
> and minds through Christ Jesus.
> —PHILIPPIANS 4:6–7, NKJV

> And my God shall supply all your need according to
> His riches in glory by Christ Jesus.
> —PHILIPPIANS 4:19, NKJV

Here is the news flash: God has not called us to do that which we can do. He has called us to do that which we could never do in a million years. *Praying through* means to believe God despite the obstacles.

I have discovered that God wants to give each of us power encounters in the area of our finances. He wants to show Himself there. This means we must extravagantly give, trust, and receive. This is living by faith, and when we do this, Jesus shows up. Ultimately He wants to show Himself to us as the source of our provision.

One of the most basic and life-altering teachings of Jesus is that we ultimately need to choose between God and money (Matt. 6:24). This doesn't apply just to the wealthy, and this doesn't mean it is wrong to be wealthy. The Bible says the love of money, not money itself, is the root of all kinds of evil (1 Tim. 6:10). The temptation to put our trust and hope in money goes right to the core of our hearts. But Jesus really can be your everything. He can be trusted much more than money.

THE GIFT OF FAITH

Bob Weiner has led many movements of revival, campus ministry, and church planting over the years. I appreciate him so much. He told me as I was planning the National Mall gathering, "You don't have a money issue; you have a faith issue. Call me anytime you need prayer for more faith." Believe me,

I took him up on that a few times, and he prayed that I would receive the gift of faith.

Faith is believing God. It is not mental gymnastics. It is not working up a feeling that something is going to happen. In fact our feelings lag behind our faith. We are overcomers by faith, even if it takes a while for us to feel victorious in a particular circumstance. Faith is to believe God's promises above our circumstances. This was a lesson I had to learn in this journey, a lesson that did not come easily.

I was so encouraged to hear one of the greatest teachers on faith say that often he thinks something God has said can't be true, but he chooses to speak God's promises back to Him in prayer and make choices that line up with what God has said. This is faith. This will move mountains. Speak the promises of God aloud to God and to your own heart, and thank Him for them. Then make decisions based on God's promises, not simply on what you perceive or feel. "We walk by faith, not by sight" (2 Cor. 5:7, NKJV).

Most of God's promises are clearly written in the Scriptures. You don't need a prophecy over your life to discover them. There are many promises of God that would be utterly life-changing if we would speak them and live as if we believed they were a reality in our lives. But there are also things God will speak personally to you that you can be confident in, whether or not you can see how they will come to pass.

Having faith like this will unlock destiny. It will open up a supernatural outflow in your life. It is never our lack of resources that hinders us. It is simply unbelief. There is no risk if God has spoken.

Chapter 8

POSSESSING NOTHING

They have no security, no possessions to call their own, not even a foot of earth to call their home, no earthly society to claim their absolute allegiance. Nay more, they have no spiritual power, experience or knowledge to afford them consolation or security. For his sake they have lost all....Yet...*theirs* is the kingdom of heaven. That kingdom dawns on *them*.

—Dietrich Bonhoeffer, *The Cost of Discipleship*

WHEN JESUS TAUGHT a crowd for the very first time, He opened His sermon by declaring one of the most important truths about how to find your place in God's story: "Blessed are the poor in spirit, for theirs is the kingdom of heaven" (Matt. 5:3).

I've heard it said that this sentence, the first line of the Sermon on the Mount, may be the most profound statement about the culture of Jesus' kingdom that has ever been made. To be poor in spirit is to know that you have nothing in yourself apart from Jesus that can produce goodness. Those who are poor in spirit are aware of the gap between what they are walking in and all God has for them. And this awareness is where our story truly begins.

You don't host Jesus' presence in your community by becoming hyperspiritual and trying harder to fix yourself; in fact the door is open only to those who know they can't fix themselves—those at the bottom of the barrel, not at the top. This doesn't mean you have to be poor financially, but it does mean the way into Jesus' kingdom is through your awareness of your total dependence on Him alone to meet your need.

Jesus did not come to make your personality a little better. He came to introduce you to the real you through death to yourself and resurrection life in Him. When Jesus invites you in, as He is doing right now, He invites you to relinquish complete control of your life to find His life. You are crucified with Him, and yet you live—but it's no longer you but Christ living in you (Gal. 2:20).

THE END AND THE BEGINNING OF A MINISTRY

Let me take you back some more years to illustrate this point. I grew up on the fringes of spiritual things in church environments, but as a teenager I was frequently bored with God even while I was around Him.

My father and mother, Scott and Sue Bradshaw, decided early on that they would expose my younger sister, Jen, and me to God's presence. So they took us with them as they travelled around the nation to the places they heard there was a move of the Spirit. I actually saw miracles firsthand, yet I was still bored with God. But something began to stir in my heart, probably because of the prayers of my amazing mother and father and their faithfulness.

I began to feel a need for God and a desire to know Him in an authentic way. This is part of what it means to be poor in spirit. Do you feel in your heart the painful gap between who Jesus is and where you are currently in your life with Him? This is not a bad thing—this is an amazing thing. It's a gift. Honestly I was getting more and more desperate by the day, and that hunger was just the beginning.

I was fifteen years old when our youth pastors took a group of teen leaders on a trip to an Assemblies of God church in Pensacola, Florida, where apparently God was spending some time. It was the craziest thing because we had to wait twelve hours in line to get into a service. They say you don't have to advertise a fire. Well, that twelve-hour line was proof of that to me. Who waits in line for twelve hours to get into a church gathering? Well, we did.

That night I lay on the red carpet of this church building in Florida, wondering why I was there and if God even knew my name. You see, I prayed probably hundreds of times for Jesus to reveal Himself to me in a personal way. I don't want you to think that I lived in some kind of spiritual utopia and just automatically felt God around me at all times. I was as confused and lost as many others have been. I had many existential questions. Most people feel so weak and vulnerable and, if they are honest, spend a large amount of their time trying to cover up that little child on the inside who is desperately searching for God. But Jesus doesn't say to cover that up. He wants to come into the mess. He wants to encounter us even in our weakness— dare I say, especially in our weakness.

That night at the church in Pensacola I had a new level of desperation. I remember pounding my fist on the red carpet and silently saying to God, "If You don't meet me, I'm gonna die." I got up, and as I was walking out of the church building, I was a bit saddened by the feeling of God's absence. It was then that a man approached me; he was wearing a little badge indicating that he was on the ministry team. I don't know this man's name to this day, but his simple question was just what I needed at that moment. "Can I pray for you?" he asked. I said yes but was careful to explain that I had been prayed for many times by many people even that very night.

What happened next remains one of the most amazing moments of my life. It felt as if thousands of volts of electricity were going through my body, but it wasn't painful. What I was feeling was the presence of God. This went on for quite some time. I completely lost track of my surroundings and time. It was like liquid love pouring over me. It wasn't just that I was baptized in the Holy Spirit that night. It was that God heard my voice. That changed everything for me. That night God showed me He was real and that He was anything but boring.

You may or may not have had an experience like I had that night. But one thing I know for sure: Jesus loves to show Himself to people who have nothing—people who are desperate and know it. This is the starting point for hosting God's presence. Everyone is qualified except those who think they have it all without God.

A few days later back in Virginia I was in someone's basement with a small group of guys from our church. One young man asked for prayer. "Sure," I figured. "After all, everything has just changed. Why not try to pray for someone else?"

I began to pray for this kid, and to all of our extreme surprise the very same thing that happened to me in Florida happened again in that basement. This time the whole group of young people experienced it, and it lasted for hours.

There was another small group of youth meeting across town. Someone called them and said, "You've got to get over here." So the other group drove across town and joined us. A few moms came because some of the kids present were barely fourteen years old and needed to be picked up. One of the moms got halfway down the stairs to the basement and froze. Then she turned around and ran back up the stairs. I asked her later why she ran back up the stairs, and she said that when she was about halfway down the stairs, she realized the presence of God was so strong that if she went into that basement, she would never come out, and she had to go meet her husband by a certain time.

This was the beginning of the end of our youth ministry as we knew it. Soon hundreds of kids from all over our region were coming to our gatherings. Our meeting location shifted to a former art gallery in downtown Fredericksburg called Mars Hill. Every Friday night hundreds of mostly fifteen-to-twenty-five-year-olds gathered with no agenda other than to pursue the one thing David wrote about in Psalm 27:4.

We wanted more of God. We didn't know we were stepping into an ancient dream. We worshipped for hours, not because we had to or because it was on the schedule for our youth group every week. We were hungry. And that hunger led us to start writing songs, praying for the sick, and talking for long hours about all that God was doing. We were having the time of our lives. We had made the great discovery David had made so many years before. One day with Him is better than a thousand elsewhere.

I am quite sure that we broke the fire code for the building occupancy at the time. Kids and adults alike just wanted to come every Friday to worship. Though we started as just a group of youth from one church, kids from all over the city were joining us, some of whom didn't even know Jesus yet. The primary tenants of the building were running a brilliant ministry from that space during the week. They had graciously been letting us use the building, but understandably there was a limit. We were packing hundreds of youth into a space that was designed to fit far fewer. Even the parking lot was full of people every Friday night! And it was loud.

These very kind people were planning to suggest we find another location for our gatherings. They went to a conference and had planned to talk to us about the need to make a change when they returned. But at this conference a prophetic man who had never met them before called them out and said, "You have a building. I see young people coming and filling it. They are coming for music, but they are encountering Jesus. God says, 'It's Me. Let them do it.'"

Well, they didn't ask us to leave. We didn't even know for years that God had intervened for a ragtag group of kids who were giving themselves to pursuing Jesus in that little former art gallery in downtown Fredericksburg.

None of us really knew what to do because it was outside of our boxes. It wasn't a church plant. It was the launching point of what has become the Awaken the Dawn movement. But at that time becoming a movement was not on our minds, and that is exactly how it was supposed to be. We were quite preoccupied with Jesus.

THE SCUM OF THE EARTH

I share this story to say that God is not inviting the wisest, most gifted, or strongest. God uses the weak things of the world to confound the wise (1 Cor. 1:27). He uses those who don't have it all figured out on the front end. He comes to those who are poor. He comes to a basement full of kids who only know they want more of Jesus.

So hosting Jesus in your community begins in poverty of spirit. If you are weak and you know it, then you are qualified.

Those who are poor in spirit no longer possess even their own lives. They are fully God's. This is an unbelievable freedom. Imagine if you no longer had to worry about your life. Imagine if nothing you own was really your possession. You don't own your money. You don't own your relationships. You don't own your ministry. You don't own your vocation. You don't own your own life. When you come to Jesus, you let go of everything, yet you possess everything.

What would it be like if you no longer had to worry about your reputation ever again? What would it look like if you never had to worry about there being enough money to do what God has called you to do? What would your life look like if all you had was Jesus, the One in whom you'll find everything you could ever need. If you truly let go of everything else to grab hold of Jesus, you could live with an absolutely free heart.

Rolland Baker expressed it this way:

I...always wanted to believe and live the Sermon on the Mount, but I was usually told that it did not mean all that I thought it meant and that I needed to be practical. I would read Scriptures longingly, trying to imagine how wonderful it would be not to worry about anything....We could always give and never lose. We could be lied to, cheated and stolen from, and yet we would always come out ahead. We would never have to take advantage of anyone or have any other motive but to bless other people. Rather than always making contingency plans in case Jesus didn't do anything, we could count on Him continually. We, our lives and all that we preach and provide would not be for sale, but would be given freely, just as we have received freely.[1]

He is more than enough—the greatest prize. The apostle Paul wrote:

> But whatever were gains to me I now consider loss for the sake of Christ. What is more, I consider everything a loss because of the surpassing worth of knowing Christ Jesus my Lord, for whose sake I have lost all things. I consider them garbage, that I may gain Christ and be found in him.
>
> —PHILIPPIANS 3:7–9

Paul told the church at Corinth that he had "become the scum of the earth, the garbage of the world," and that they should imitate him (1 Cor. 4:13, 16). In Jesus' kingdom lower is always higher. Your true freedom lies not in self-promotion but in getting under others, lifting them up, and exalting Jesus.

If we're going to have even a discussion about seeing Jesus' transformational presence fill campuses and cities, we have to start with this basic truth. We have nothing in ourselves. But Jesus comes and asks for all of our nothing, and then gives us His everything.

Today you can be free. You can be free from the anxiety that is gripping the earth as a result of political and sociological issues. You can be free from being defined by failure or weakness. You can now be on the journey to live with Jesus.

Chapter 9

BECOMING A VOICE

A voice of one calling: "In the wilderness prepare the way for the LORD; make straight in
the desert a highway for our God."

—ISAIAH 40:3

I T IS MY belief that one of the greatest mysteries of Jesus' life is His silent years. He spent the first thirty years of His life doing no miracles, teaching no crowds, leading nothing. He was a carpenter's son, a working man—a man who never married and had no children of His own. It is almost unthinkable that God walked the earth for thirty years and did not reveal Himself.

We are so often in a hurry, and God is interested in quality over quantity. Jesus' silent years are proof of that. Most of the time when we have a vision from God, there are delays in the process, and that is part of God's genius.

As John Ortberg wrote, "For many of us the great danger is not that we will renounce our faith. It is that we will become so distracted and rushed and preoccupied that we will settle for a mediocre version of it. We will just skim our lives instead of actually living them."[1]

What did Jesus do for thirty years? We know this: "And Jesus grew in wisdom and stature, and in favor with God and man" (Luke 2:52). Jesus was growing in intimacy with God— He was learning to commune with God as a man. Though He was fully God, He still had to grow into His intimacy with God as a flesh-and-blood man.

In my mind that means He was eating up the Bible and learning to pray. The only account we have of Jesus during this

84

time of His life is when He was in the temple as a young man, shocking the teachers of the Law with His questions and understanding of the Scriptures (Luke 2:41–51).

Even after His thirty years of relative silence, He immediately went to the desert after John baptized Him and spent forty days at the beginning of His public ministry fasting, praying, and being tested. So Jesus' thirty silent years were immediately followed by forty days of fasting in the wilderness.

During this time, Jesus was becoming a voice.

And what happened when Jesus opened His mouth to speak to the masses? Matthew's Gospel says, "The crowds were amazed at his teaching, because he taught as one who had authority, and not as their teachers of the law" (Matt. 7:28–29).

Total obedience and a life of prayer, fasting, and communion with God is the greenhouse that produces voices—those who have something to say that carries the authority of heaven and brings change. The world is an echo chamber longing for clear voices. God wants to use you to host Jesus' presence in your city or on your campus. But He's not looking for those who simply repeat mantras they have heard others say. He's looking for those who will invest the time to seek Jesus' face for themselves and hear His voice. Before we speak, we need to hear. And in God's world this takes time.

Refined in the Wilderness

So what we need is the wilderness. I don't mean going to the actual desert necessarily. I mean creating time and space in our lives to remove all the distractions of busyness and listen to God. I am convinced that the rush to get a platform, lead a ministry, or appear successful is one of the greatest hindrances to what God wants to do in our lives. God is not in a hurry. In fact He says His yoke is easy and His burden is light (Matt.

11:30). Effectiveness in ministry is not born in striving; it's born in intimacy.

Paul knew on day one of his salvation that he was going to go to the whole world with the gospel because Jesus told him so in that Damascus road encounter. Most scholars believe it was about fourteen years later before he was finally launched out on his first missionary journey. What did he do for fourteen years?

Paul "went into" the wilderness of Arabia before going to Jerusalem after his conversion. He literally went to the desert (Gal. 1:16–17, ESV). He delayed going to Jerusalem for three years, during which time he developed a lifestyle of communing with God that spilled over into the rest of his ministry. In one of his letters to the Thessalonians, Paul spoke of being "entrusted with the gospel" (1 Thess. 2:4). Oh, that God would raise up a generation that is entrusted with the gospel!

John the Baptist spent most of his life in the desert, searching the Scriptures and learning to pray. He most likely spent only six to nine months in public ministry, but by the time he emerged from that wilderness, all of Israel came to hear him talk. We have no record that he did any miracles, so those crowds gathered to hear what John had to say. John didn't simply repeat what he heard others teaching or saying. He spoke the message God had given him, born out of this communion with God. He was a voice, not an echo, and you can be too.

In fact John identified himself as a voice, quoting the prophet Isaiah when he said, "I am the voice of one calling in the wilderness, 'Make straight the way for the Lord'" (John 1:23). John had studied the Scriptures so much that he found himself there!

In the third and fourth centuries there was a group of people called the desert fathers and mothers. They were men and women who went into the wilderness for long seasons to focus on prayer and fasting and to give themselves to knowing Jesus. Some of them became amazing voices. Some of them were a bit off. I don't think most of us are supposed to sell everything and move to the desert, but I do think we all need the wilderness in our lives. We need to give time to a private pursuit of God's face. This is how you become a voice instead of an echo!

This is the key: anyone can live a secret life of prayer, fasting, and studying the Word of God. If you will make this investment, God will do what He excels in doing. He will cause eternity to echo through your life. Your voice and life will have authority. This is open to anyone; it is not limited to preachers. Your voice matters in God's plan.

Many of us need to slow down, put our ears on Jesus' chest, and listen for His heartbeat. Like John the Baptizer we can become a voice for our generation. Our message? Just like John's, it will be who Jesus is and what He is going to do.

TOTAL OBEDIENCE

Throughout these pages we have talked about the key to hosting Jesus' presence being a context of worship and prayer. I believe there is another essential key: total obedience to Jesus. It is in our obedience that we become voices.

Connecting total obedience to Jesus with our increased experience of His presence and ability to walk in His will for our lives was a life-changing revelation to me. I will say it clearly: total obedience is essential to hosting Jesus' presence and walking in His story. Most people try to obey God because they fear negative consequences. It's true that there are consequences for disregarding Jesus' teaching. But we were never meant to live primarily from a place of fear of negative consequences. We were designed to live for love. When we are able to see obedience as directly connected to our ability to host Jesus' presence and walk out the amazing destiny God has for us, obedience becomes freeing to the human heart, and we happily obey.

This is why I believe the heart values Jesus articulated in the

Sermon on the Mount are the starting point for living with Jesus. Beginning with the eight Beatitudes, the Sermon on the Mount tells us what a happy and Christ-soaked life looks like. Jesus said this very directly:

> Whoever has my commands and keeps them is the one who loves me. The one who loves me will be loved by my Father, and I too will love them and show myself to them.
>
> —JOHN 14:21

In this passage Jesus told us that our love for Him looks like obedience to Him. But the fact that Jesus ties our obedience to His showing Himself to us gives a greater understanding of why obedience is much more an expression of love than a fear-based means of avoiding punishment.

Jesus is saying that as you surrender yourself to Him and say yes to Him with 100 percent of your heart and will, your experience of His presence in and around your life will increase—guaranteed. It is not that Jesus is saying we are earning more of Him. This is true because He is love.

You see, Jesus cannot bless us if we are living in a way that is harmful to ourselves, others, and His name. He loves us too much to allow that, and He is committed to authenticity, the very thing so many people today are hungry for. Disobedience to Jesus is not a disregard for a set of principles; it is actually a rejection of Jesus personally, because He has invested Himself personally in us. As image bearers of God we are affected by our disobedience but so are the people around us and even creation itself. As love incarnate God cannot allow that which hinders love to rule in our lives or in creation, because it represents death to that which is beautiful and good. Obeying Jesus is not optional for those who want to host His presence. The intensity of His love demands 100 percent obedience, not partial obedience.

When I say 100 percent obedience, I am not talking about never making a mistake. We are still growing. When we fail (notice I said when, not if) and turn to God, He is not angry with us. This is why Jesus died—to heal us. So the issue is not that we fail but what we do when we are unsuccessful in our commitment to 100 percent obedience: whether we turn to Him in repentance and recommit to total obedience or shrink back into a place of compromise. God is incredibly patient with us. In fact He is helping us—that's how much He wants us to repent and turn to Him.

God's demand for total obedience does not mean that when we struggle with a sin or habit we are disqualified from hosting Jesus' presence and becoming a voice in God's kingdom. In fact that couldn't be further from the truth. The grace of God enables us to struggle and engage the process of repentance and restoration from a place of victory. Stumbling or falling as we are giving ourselves to 100 percent obedience to Jesus is very different from rebellion. Rebellion is when we make a commitment at the heart level to disobey Jesus or when we stop caring about what He says. The reality is that many of us are still growing in our obedience. But when we give God a hard-and-fast no (an act of rebellion), we are embracing a toxic lifestyle that ultimately leads to self-destruction.

Here is the challenging reality: to live in intentional compromise over time means we are not on the path of life. You cannot knowingly say no to Jesus on an ongoing basis and actually be saved. This is because in His love God cannot allow a person with this posture to be in His kingdom since it destroys us, His name, and many others around us.

This is why love and obedience are forever joined together. God loves us, wants the best for us, and shows us the way to become all that we were meant to be. But our choices do matter forever, and we can choose the opposite of love.

Jesus assists us in this journey by helping us to understand that the main reason to obey Him is that in obedience we find ourselves, we find Him, and we experience His presence in new and profound ways that are life changing both for us and for those around us.

David, the man after God's own heart who desired to host God's presence in his life and in Israel, said, "I will ponder the way that is blameless. Oh when will you come to me? I will walk with integrity of heart within my house" (Ps. 101:2, ESV). He connected total obedience directly to God coming to him. When you see obedience through this lens, the question becomes not, "What can I get away with?" but, "How far can I go in love?"

Jesus is a Bridegroom. Can you imagine a bride telling her husband she will be faithful to him 95 percent of the time? We all know that would never really work in a marriage. One hundred percent faithfulness is the only way to really live.

Marital love, like our love for God, was designed for exclusivity. Because God is love and has given us all of His heart, He asks and expects all of our hearts. This includes even the things we love most.

Beautiful Surrender

I want to share a personal story that I believe will illustrate this point. Many years ago I met a girl. Truthfully I fell completely in love with her. There are few things that affect the human heart like romantic relationships. At that time, as is typical of eighteen-year-olds, all I could think about was our relationship. This is perfectly natural and normal. But I began to have this nagging thought that I was more passionately committed to that relationship than I was to God Himself.

When you're at the height of a newfound romantic interest, I think it's quite normal to have overwhelming feelings that can seem to trump everything else, including what you might feel toward God at that specific moment. I don't believe this is wrong. But what I was feeling wasn't just the euphoria of that time—it was something deeper, and I could not shake it. I felt in my heart the finger of the Holy Spirit messing with something that I really didn't want Him to touch. He was exposing something to me about myself, which was that while I talked a lot about God at that time, Jesus had yet to become my whole life.

Maybe this sounds extreme. As I mentioned, the euphoric experiences associated with falling in love were designed by Jesus Himself. They are not to be despised as simply carnal. But I knew at the end of the day that my relationship with this person was more important to me than anything else. You see, when Jesus calls us, He calls us to come and die so we can truly live again.

I knew I needed to step away from this girl for whom I had the strongest of feelings. For me it was like God asking Abraham to sacrifice Isaac. Just as God instructed Abraham to give up his son as a test of his heart, I knew I needed to give up the one relationship in my life that meant more to me than anything. I could not live with the reality that my love for Jesus was half-hearted. And by half-hearted I don't just mean in the realm of my feelings; it was in my core sense of identity. Where I was finding my true life is what was in question at that time. You should be thankful if God keeps you on a short leash.

The thing that made this even more unusual was that I spent the previous six months praying on a daily basis, oftentimes numerous times a day, for God to make this specific relationship beautiful. I prayed for Jesus to take full possession of even this part of my life. So when the thought began to come that I should lay the relationship down and embark on a journey of total yielding, I tried as hard as I could to shake it. I fought it. Interestingly she was having similar feelings at the same time. We both knew something needed to shift in our hearts and perhaps in our relationship.

We decided we would both pray separately and ask the Lord how to move forward in a healthy way. After that week of praying, we each felt very strongly that we needed to lay down our relationship without any expectation that we would pick it up again. This was one of the hardest things I've ever done. With many tears we laid down the relationship. Shortly thereafter she decided to move with her family to Alabama.

For the next two years, we lost touch. We didn't see each other or have any serious conversation after she moved. We didn't know what was happening in each other's life, nor did we pursue finding out. The relationship was completely over as far as we were both concerned. I will confess that I often wondered why I would have prayed numerous times a day for six months for God to bless our relationship if it was going to completely die. But here is my testimony to you. During that two-year period of time, I discovered a life with Jesus that far transcended anything I'd ever tasted. I was completely ruined for anything less. I am not exaggerating. I began to experience personal moments with God that marked me in ways words fail to express. I later discovered that she was also learning some important things and having some powerful experiences with the Lord.

Then a few years after she moved to Alabama, on a cold December day she came back to Virginia to visit her friends. At that time, I was in the height of this experience of satisfaction with Jesus that actually led me—half jokingly and half seriously—to tell others I thought I would likely remain single like Paul. I didn't feel like I needed anything else anymore. I was in love with God and satisfied by His presence. So I was not looking for a relationship at that particular time.

Since she was in town and we had been friends for a long time before, I decided that maybe we should catch up over a quick lunch. We had both been on a wild journey over the previous few years and had completely lost touch. So I asked her if she had any time during her visit to grab lunch. She agreed. We set a date for the next day to meet at a local bagel shop. That lunch was one of the craziest experiences of my life. I did not see what was coming. Though I couldn't tell you what either of us ordered that day, I will never forget the moment she got up to go use the restroom.

I was sitting at the table of the restaurant by myself after an amazing conversation, and it was like a Mack Truck hit me. I couldn't stop thinking about her and the conversation we just had. It felt surreal. I was in shock. I was completely and totally in love with her instantly. I had barely thought about her for the last couple of years, and here I was feeling a euphoric, passionate desire for her that was even stronger and purer than when we were together before. Within months we were married. Marrying Ashley was the best choice I've ever made outside of giving my life to Jesus. In our case God resurrected our Isaac. He did the exact thing I asked Him to do during that six-month period of time years earlier. He made our relationship beautiful—in His timing.

We were born to dream with God. We were born to see His presence fill our lives, communities, and nations. However, living from this basic posture of total surrender to Jesus sometimes involves laying down those very dreams, even the ones that come from God, and resting in a place of complete trust. Many times God will take you into a season that looks like the very opposite of the thing that you're hearing and believing for. This is where trust comes in, because those who hope in the Lord will never be put to shame (Ps. 25:3).

You can't lose when you lose everything in Him. It's impossible to miss out when Jesus is at the wheel of your life. Frankly there are times when our desires become one of the best indicators of God's will for our lives, because the Lord is so good He loves to dream with us and give us the desires of our hearts. But He is jealous and committed to staying our foremost desire. That's why David said, "Delight yourself in the LORD, and he will give you the desires of your heart" (Ps. 37:4, ESV).

Are you willing to give Jesus everything in your life, especially the good parts? The reality is this: when you surrender your life to God, laying down even good things that you suspect are not the best things, you can be guaranteed of this one thing—God brings only beauty from your surrender. He will give you something better. But above all else He gives you Himself.

What we need now are voices, not echoes. This comes in our total surrender to Jesus and our communion with Him. This is not to suggest that we are all going to be saying different things or that our messages are somehow disconnected from sound doctrine and orthodoxy. It means we are speaking from revelation in our hearts born from the context of intimacy with Jesus. Voices will bring transformation, not hype. You are invited to become a voice in this generation.

PART III

TOGETHER CULTURE

Chapter 10

A CREATIVE RENAISSANCE

The anointing the Lord is about to release on music is going to sweep the world in a manner like the Beatles did when they first came out. It's going to be a music that is new in kind, new in sound, arresting in its content; it will stop traffic, and it will turn men's heads and capture their hearts, but this time it will do it for the Lord.

—JAMES RYLE

"IT'S LIKE A distant thunder," I sang, the lyrics and melody pouring out spontaneously. "I can hear it coming closer, closer…" The musicians behind me were playing spontaneously, moving as the Spirit led us, and the music was hitting a crescendo. Then just when the song was at its most intense, lightning struck right beside our building. The lights in the room flickered, and several people let out startled shouts at the peal of thunder. The band stopped playing. For a moment we all stared at one another. We hadn't heard reports of a storm anywhere in our area. Apparently a storm had come suddenly upon us.

I am convinced God was messing with us that night. I had just finished speaking on the coming creative renaissance— that God is about to bring worshipping communities a unique expression of His presence in the midst of an explosion of new songs and sounds. In Genesis 1 God created the world with His voice, and His voice is still filled with creative power. It would be like these artists could hear the thunder that comes from God's throne (Rev. 4:5) and creatively bring the sound of heaven, the sound of God's voice and heart, to earth. Then the spontaneous song started. Then the lightning struck. I guess we have a thing with lightning—and God has a sense of humor.

One thing that has become all too clear is how important music and creativity are in God's plan. Most of us take for granted the fact that almost every time we gather with groups of believers, we sing. In culture, music and the arts bring definition to who a people are. Few have stopped to think deeply about why music and the arts have always been so central to the unfolding of God's plans and how we do life together as Jesus followers. But we must understand this connection whether or not we are musicians or artists ourselves. This relationship is far too important to ignore.

Music is more central to the church than to almost any other kind of entity. Imagine if every time you showed up for class at a university, you spent the first half of your time together singing. Imagine if you did that every single class. It would be a bizarre and unusual scholastic experience to say the least. But when we get together in various church environments, we almost always sing, even if the music is not very good.

Just about everyone appreciates music as part of the human experience, and most people are glad there's a singing portion of our gatherings. But the fact that music feels good does not explain what God is doing. Millions of people all over the world are going to be singing and writing songs in the years to come, and we must understand why God wants this to happen.

What Isaiah Saw

Something Isaiah saw over 2,500 years ago clues us into what Jesus is doing:

> *They* [the nations] *shall lift up their voice, they shall sing*; for the majesty of the LORD they shall cry aloud from the sea. Therefore glorify the LORD in the dawning light, the name of the LORD God of Israel in the coastlands of the sea. *From the ends of the earth we have heard songs: "Glory to the righteous!"*...It shall

come to pass in that day that the LORD will punish on high the host of exalted ones, and on the earth the kings of the earth.
—ISAIAH 24:14–16, 21, NKJV, EMPHASIS ADDED

Sing to the LORD a *new song*, and His praise from the ends of the earth, you who go down to the sea, and all that is in it, you coastlands and you inhabitants of them! Let the wilderness and its cities lift up their voice, the villages that Kedar inhabits. Let the inhabitants of Sela sing, let them shout from the top of the mountains. Let them give glory to the LORD, and declare His praise in the coastlands. The LORD shall go forth like a mighty man; He shall stir up His zeal like a man of war. He shall cry out, yes, shout aloud; He shall prevail against His enemies. "I have held My peace a long time, I have been still and restrained Myself. Now I will cry like a woman in labor, I will pant and gasp at once."
—ISAIAH 42:10–14, NKJV, EMPHASIS ADDED

Isaiah saw this as a fact of the future. The whole world is going to be filled with a new song and a new sound. The title of this song is going to be "Glory to the Righteous One (Jesus)," but it will take many expressions.

These verses in Isaiah are more than poetry. They are going to happen. The prophet says in cities and coastlands, in the Middle East and deserts, and even at the top of mountains, people will be singing for joy. Then, presumably in response to the songs of worship covering the earth, God will shout. We can all be quite sure that when God shouts, the world will know.

This is an actual future reality, because from the context of these verses, the timing is around the return of Jesus. This points to something that is a game changer. This movement of worship, creativity, and prayer is not going away. It will not be a fad. It is going to grow beyond anything we could have ever imagined. Because God is a lover and because music gives expression to His love and His presence, He is going to fulfill His plan through thousands of singing communities. In other words, worship and creativity are right at the center of His strategy because He inhabits the praise of His people and His actual power is released in the context of creative worship.

We host Jesus' presence by joining this dream of musicians and artists finding their voices and filling their communities, their prayer rooms, and the culture around them with a new song. The song of the Lamb is coming. This song will cover the earth, God will inhabit those praises (Ps. 22:3), and Isaiah says this will lead to Jesus' return. Jesus is not coming in a vacuum. As John proclaimed in Revelation, "The Spirit and the bride say, 'Come!'" (Rev. 22:17). The bride (the church) is going to be crying out in love and desire for Jesus to return, saying, "Come!" This prayer of love and desire for Jesus will undoubtedly be musical. Jesus is going to return in response to the songs and prayers of desire for Him that will fill the earth. He is coming as a Bridegroom.

Why is this going to happen? It has to do with God's ways, which are quite opposite of human wisdom. Only God would come up with a strategic plan that involved filling our cities and church communities with music and worship, and in that environment releasing His power and light. It is supernatural, but it also could not be more pragmatic. When God's presence and Word are released with music and worship from pure hearts, they bring profound change. Here is the simple truth: in our creative worship and adoration of Jesus, God comes down. He moves in our hearts and in our environments.

The night we started our prayer room in Virginia, we crammed about two hundred people into a room that was meant for just under one hundred. What was launched that night has continued now for many years, but we didn't know at the time the significance of that first prayer gathering. That night a friend I'll call Matt was there for the first time, and he was not following Jesus. He attended the launch as a favor to a friend he met while working at Starbucks. What makes this interesting is that he was an indie musician in our area and was fairly well-known in that scene.

We were in worship when we saw this young guy run to the front of the room and lie on the floor. Matt met Jesus that night.

I had never met him before, but Matt and I began to talk after the service. I remember him saying that he knew he could never write a worship song. He wasn't that kind of musician, he explained. Days later he approached me again. "I wrote a worship song," he said. We laughed together. Of course he did.

Later I went to one of the bars where Matt performed on a regular basis to hear him play his new song. He was as bold as a lion, telling everyone about Jesus. That experience impacted me deeply. Reflecting on Matt as I wrote this chapter made me think about what God might want to do. Matt loves Jesus to this day, and he met God in an environment of prayer and worship. That encounter not only changed Matt's life; it permeated his music. I believe there are more Matts coming, and there is much more God wants to do through artists in the future.

Making Room for the Sound of the Lord

Before I was leading prayer rooms and a movement of 24/7 worship held in tents, I was a music major at a secular university. In our music history class we studied David's tabernacle from three thousand years ago. To understand what I believe is about to take place, it is helpful to look again at David's tent.

In those days there was nothing in the world like the tent David built to house the ark of the covenant. David and his team invented instruments, wrote countless songs in the presence of

God, and employed a small army of four thousand full-time musicians (1 Chron. 9:33; 23:5). Even as king, David apparently found time to worship seven times per day (Ps. 119:164). David's worship movement defined the culture of the day.

As I studied music history, I was fascinated to discover that believers in Jesus initiated many of the significant musical advances throughout history. As a music major my first few semesters studying Western music were dedicated almost exclusively to church music. Though I am glad Christians had such a significant impact on Western music history, it is tragic that music education pays less attention to the non-Western cultural sounds. Of course there are non-Western sounds that God loves, and they are just as important to Him.

A very significant shift happened in the Western church, however, during the Protestant Reformation. Martin Luther and the reformers observed that the music of the church was not being written for congregational singing as much as for highly skilled musicians. So Luther took popular tunes of his day and wrote hymns to their melodies, putting an emphasis on the songs being easy to sing and having sound doctrine.

Something significant was gained through this, but something also was lost. The positive was that hymns were reintroduced and widely sung. The negative was that the more skilled musicians no longer had a place in the corporate gatherings of the church to reach for the fullness of their creativity. I believe God wants to restore both of these dimensions in the coming creative renaissance. The highest dimensions of creative expression should find a place in worshipping communities and impact the culture around us. I promise you that this is coming.

My point is this: the Psalms do not say to limit creativity. It's quite the opposite. It's as David wrote, "Awake, harp and lyre!" (Ps. 108:2). In other words, God is the source of creativity, and we are being conformed to His image. This will stretch some of us and break some of our boxes, but it is coming. Creating environments within church communities where the artists among us can stretch their wings, learn to minister to God, and operate with authenticity and freedom is more important to seeing heaven come to earth than we may have realized. Isaiah seems to indicate this.

To be clear, songs are coming that don't fit the normal worship "box," and this is OK. We need songs with strong choruses, songs that are biblical and easy for congregations to sing together. But we also need songs that take the reins off our creative people, no-holds-barred songs that are vertical in worship to God and allow for the full gamut of creativity. We need both, even in the context of congregational worship.

When we make space for the sounds of God in our church communities and in the culture, we are making space for God Himself. Once again, this is pragmatic and full of joy. That's the great thing about God's culture—He always marries those two things together.

A NEW SONG

It is a sad state of affairs when you have to look at the world for creative inspiration. Too many Christians operate this way, but that is going to change. Some of the greatest and most powerful creative voices are going to emerge from within worshipping communities. These creative voices are being invited to excellence. What the artists and musicians are carrying is much bigger than just self-expression. Some songs are meant primarily for worship gatherings, some are meant to engage the culture around us, and many will do both, but they all will express the song of the Lamb.

That sound you are carrying is an expression of Jesus in you, and we need it to come forth, because as you find your voice, Jesus rides on your worship and creative expression. The song God has placed in your heart will change the atmosphere in your church community. It will release Jesus' real presence in your sphere of influence, and it will position you as a cultural architect to establish values and language that shape people's perspectives. From the Beatles to Billie Eilish, there are numerous examples of the incredible influence of musicians. There is a God-given authority on musicians that can be used rightly or wrongly.

By the way, this does not mean the point of art or music is solely to preach at people. That would be disingenuous. It is an authentic expression of the heart. But when we are priests and our hearts are burning with love for our Savior, Jesus shines.

One of the most powerful prophetic words from the last few decades that has been shared and reshared is the "Sons of Thunder" prophecy from James Ryle that I quoted at the beginning of this chapter. This prophecy came as a series of dreams, and in one of the dreams Ryle saw a room on the side of a church's stage that had all kinds of unused equipment. In a corner was a dusty amplifier that turned out to be the Beatles' amplifier—the very source of their sound and power.[1]

The sound to impact nations belongs to us; it is hidden among us, waiting to be released. I want you to catch this: there is a creative renaissance coming that will be as powerful in communities as Beatlemania was in the 1960s. It will be Isaiah's song. It is what David experienced in his tent. It is the song of the Lamb.

Times are coming when songs and sounds will actually cause hearts to be awakened to what God is truly like. Bodies will be healed, people will be saved, regions and nations will be transformed, angels will move, and God will be known.

When Isaiah speaks of a "new song" (a phrase that is used multiple times in the Book of Revelation to describe what is going on in heaven), he is not speaking just about new music. He is speaking of new seasons and new works of God. Seasons of awakening and transition are always accompanied by a new song.

FREEDOM SONGS

I wonder if part of Paul's vision for singing communities (which we will discuss later in this chapter) came from his own experience. Paul experienced a literal song of deliverance in Acts 16. Paul and his ministry partner, Silas, were locked up in a Philippian jail cell for preaching the gospel. Scripture says they were singing their hearts out to God at about midnight. Apparently all the prisoners were listening. (I'm sure they were. Who sings at midnight?)

Suddenly there was an earthquake. Their worship was not only impacting the supernatural; it was stirring something in the natural around them. This was a specific kind of earthquake. It was for freedom. The cell doors opened, and everyone's chains fell off—not just Paul's and Silas' chains; all the prisoners' chains came loose. They all ended up giving their lives to Jesus, including the prison keeper.

David experienced something similar when demonic torment left Saul at the sound of David's worship (1 Sam. 16). Every time Saul was being tormented by demons, he would send for David, and as David played his harp, the demons would leave. This must have convinced David that what he had been cultivating out in the field while tending sheep was significant, because he replicated this later in his life with thousands of musicians.

David trained musicians by the thousands to prophesy on their instruments. What would happen if we taught musicians the same skill today?

Look at what happened in David's tabernacle:

> Moreover David and the captains of the army separated for the service some of the sons of Asaph, of

> Heman, and of Jeduthun, who should prophesy with
> harps, stringed instruments, and cymbals. And the
> number of the skilled men performing their service
> was: Of the sons of Asaph: Zaccur, Joseph, Nethaniah,
> and Asharelah; the sons of Asaph were under the
> direction of Asaph, who prophesied according to the
> order of the king. Of Jeduthun, the sons of Jeduthun:
> Gedaliah, Zeri, Jeshaiah, Shimei, Hashabiah, and
> Mattithiah, six, under the direction of their father
> Jeduthun, who prophesied with a harp to give thanks
> and to praise the LORD.
> —1 CHRONICLES 25:1–3, NKJV

This tells me the sounds and songs that come in God's presence carry something more than just music and lyrics. They express God's heart, His life, His actual voice. He reveals Himself and His presence in our worship.

David taught others what he had learned, which means we can learn this too. He taught the importance of seeing and hearing. It is like a sacred intuition. Learning to connect to what God is doing with a group of people and give it expression will change those people's mindsets. Musicians are naturally feelers, but mostly they feel what is going on in themselves. This is valid and needed because expressing ourselves to God is good. But there is a place where we can feel what God is doing and give it sound. This, then, becomes an expression of God's voice, which again has creative ability just as it did in Genesis 1 when God said, "Let there be light," and light came into being (v. 3).

This is similar to what the prophet Elisha experienced. He said, "'But now bring me a musician.' And when the musician played, the hand of the LORD came upon him. And he said, 'Thus says the LORD'" (2 Kings 3:15–16, ESV). A sound enabled the prophet to receive from heaven.

Heaven is filled with singing. The primary leaders all have

harps in their hands (Rev. 5:8), and angels are constantly singing. God surrounds Himself with songs, sounds, colors, light, thunderings, and joy. And this is not a light show. It is glory.

This is what is coming to a city near you. Jesus' sound explosion is on the horizon. This is why we need to release, support, fund, and champion creatives among us.

The Power of Corporate Worship

I don't believe the apostle Paul could sing well. Obviously I don't know this, but no one gets all the gifts. Perhaps not being able to sing was his thorn in the flesh. (I'm just kidding.)

However, despite (possibly) being unable to sing, Paul told believers to do that very thing:

> And do not be drunk with wine, in which is dissipation; but be filled with the Spirit, speaking to one another in psalms and hymns and spiritual songs, singing and making melody in your heart to the Lord, giving thanks always for all things to God the Father in the name of our Lord Jesus Christ, submitting to one another in the fear of God.
> —Ephesians 5:18–21, nkjv

> Let the word of Christ dwell in you richly in all wisdom, teaching and admonishing one another in psalms and hymns and spiritual songs, singing with grace in your hearts to the Lord.
> —Colossians 3:16, nkjv

Paul wasn't writing these words to singers; he was saying this to everyone. I believe this is because he knew what would happen when the church embraced singing as a constant part of our lives together.

Paul was a genius at building the church, and while it may come as a surprise to some, he used the same principles as

David. Paul told us this, and it has produced a two-thousand-year-old musical movement that has impacted the whole world. Paul was essentially building the same worship movement as David when he made singing normative in churches.

There are two reasons Paul told us to sing together:

1. We are filled with the Holy Spirit when we sing together.

2. We are filled with the Word of God when we sing together.

We will feel God's presence more intimately and know His Word and His will *as we sing*. This is why Paul insisted on singing in church gatherings. This results in more power and breakthrough. Our experience of God increases as we *sing*, not simply as we read or study the Bible (though that is extremely important as well).

In the passages quoted previously, Paul mentioned three kinds of singing that we are still called to employ.

1. Psalms—This refers to singing from the Bible. Paul knew that singing the Scriptures not only engages our intellects but touches every part of our beings, including our spirits and emotions. So the Word begins to dwell in us as we encounter Jesus in the Word through song. This is a powerful type of song that we use often in our prayer room. At times we sing directly from the Bible, and at other times we will unpack a verse through spontaneous singing.

2. Hymns—Hymns are prewritten songs that emphasize theology or are expressions of praise and intimacy with God. I classify all of our

prewritten worship songs as hymns. These are the songs we typically put on the screens to sing corporately in our church gatherings.

3. Spiritual songs—This is perhaps the most over-looked dimension of singing in the church. The Greek phrase translated "spiritual songs" is *ōdē pneumatikos*, which essentially means "Spirit song."[2] This refers to spontaneous singing with the Holy Spirit's help, much like singing in the spirit. This was a normal part of life in the early church, and it should be a typical part of our church communities as well.

The same principles apply to videographers, graphic designers, social media influencers, and other creatives. The first group of people the Bible says were filled with the Holy Spirit were the artisans who built the tabernacle (Exod. 28:3). But this shouldn't be surprising. From God's throne come color, lightning, thunder, and various sounds. This is what He sur-rounds Himself with. I believe a media movement is coming. Just like the artists of old who built a dwelling place for God in the tabernacle, web designers, songwriters, videographers, photographers, and the like will be collectively building Jesus a place where He can show up and show off. Get ready.

God is working in the hearts of leaders. So if you are creative and feel stifled by your church community, be patient and stay connected to your local church. Your leaders may not be where you are creatively, but honor them. God cares about the dream of your heart, and He is working both in their hearts and in yours to release the creative expression He has placed within His people.

Pure Worship

In order to see Isaiah 42 and 24 fulfilled, creatives have to learn how to move God's heart. This is what David understood. In order for this to happen, a certain kind of performance mindset really cannot endure. Performance at its core is all about getting attention for yourself. This is not to say God is not calling people to make albums or to play music in different venues. It is to say that creative people need to become priests first and stay in that position.

Do you know who the father of all who play instruments is? Genesis 4:21 tells us his name was Jubal. He was in the lineage of Cain, the man who killed his brother, Abel, out of jealousy because Abel's offering was pure and his was not. In other words, there is jealousy in the lineage of musicians. The whole music industry is plagued with obsessive self-promotion and leveraging everyone toward the goals of fame and notoriety. This is the lineage of Cain. If we are going to touch what Isaiah saw, step one is to have purity of heart. It is to finally lay to rest the competition and operate in a very different heart posture. Creativity will thrive when it is not driven by comparison as much as by love and authenticity.

If you are a musician reading this, you may need to get by yourself, at home rather than on a stage, and play until you feel God's presence. Learn to do that, and your songs will carry a power talent alone will never produce.

Regardless of what type of creative you are, ask yourself if you'd be content if your best work was reserved for God alone to enjoy and no one but the Lord ever heard or saw it. That is a difficult proposition, partly because creativity is designed to communicate to others, but it does point to something at the heart level of worshippers. To get to the place where you can give God your worship as an offering of love and not as a way to show your giftedness will take your creative expression to an even higher place than you can dream.

We need everyone's voice in worship. Some are called to influence large numbers of people and, perhaps, to have a large platform. But thousands upon thousands of songs are going to flood the earth. There are many Davids singing to God alone on the hillside. Though they are unknown, their voices are just as important as anyone with prominence and fame. It's time to champion those Davids and see our communities filled with the songs of the Lamb, because as we do this, we will be progressing in hosting Jesus' presence. May He be our song.

Chapter 11

JESUS' PROTEST MOVEMENT

This is no weekend war that we'll walk away
from and forget about in a couple of hours.
This is for keeps, a life-or-death fight to the
finish against the Devil and all his angels.

—EPHESIANS 6:12, MSG

A T A TIME when protest culture is gripping our society, I think it's important to understand that Jesus loves justice. The key is that He brings it through our prayers.

In Luke 18:1–8 Jesus told the story of a persistent widow. Seeking justice against her adversary, the widow kept going before an unjust judge, crying out for him to respond. In the end the judge made sure the woman got justice because she kept bothering him. Through this parable Jesus was telling us to pray and not give up, because when we cry out day and night, justice comes quickly (v. 7). Justice means wrong things are made right, and God does this through His people.

Although I don't agree with everything the late theologian Walter Wink wrote, I love this statement he made about the power of intercession:

> Intercessory prayer is spiritual defiance of what is, in the name of what God has promised. Intercession visualizes an alternative future to the one apparently fated by the momentum of current forces. Prayer infuses the air of a time yet to be into the suffocating atmosphere of the present. History belongs to the intercessors who believe the future into being.[1]

Can you visualize what God wants to do in a group of people or circumstance? Your voice can become the change agent. Things are not supposed to stay the way they are. As you pray for God's heart and will to become your own, His burden for justice will grow inside you, and as you give it voice, God's dreams will become a reality on earth as they are in heaven.

A Serial Rapist and Prayers for Justice

We had been hosting the presence of Jesus through worship and prayer for some time when the Lord began showing us that He wanted us to be spiritually defiant, to use Wink's phrase, through prayer. This became crystal clear to us after a small prayer gathering we had one night.

That particular night, five people shared that they had dreams the previous night about sexual abuse taking place in our region. This was striking to me: five different people dreamed about the same thing on the same night. We immediately changed our plans since we knew that God speaks through dreams and when we talk to Him, He talks back. So we prayed that night for God to intervene right then for victims of sexual abuse in our region. We had no idea in our natural minds where or when this abuse was happening. But it couldn't be an accident that five people had similar dreams on the same night and that all five people were in the same prayer gathering.

The next morning, I was driving to our prayer room when I turned on the news and heard that the previous night while we were praying, police had arrested a serial rapist in northern Virginia who had tragically assaulted numerous women over about a two-week period. Roughly forty-five miles from where our little group had been praying, a serial rapist had been apprehended just hours after we began to intercede. This is speedy justice. How many people in the greater DC area were protected from further harm because a little group of people created an environment where God could talk to them, they could pray about what He said, and things could change?

CRAZY FAVOR

Intercession is less about issues and more about real people. God wants to save, heal, and change people. Truth be told, the greatest tool you have for loving people is your prayers. Yes, we are to love people with our words and deeds, but we have more ability to love people in prayer than anywhere else. You can unleash a whirlwind of God's love and activity around someone's life by praying for the person. Your words have incredible power with God.

Who are you praying for regularly? If you begin to regularly pray God's will for others, you will find God's favor on your life. God is looking for those who will focus on others even more than themselves. Become a person of prayer for others—for individuals and groups in your city, your church, or the nations. Do this, and you will find God's favor in and around your life. This is what Jesus modeled. He laid aside His privileges to give His entire life for others. It is because Jesus voluntarily humbled Himself that God lifted Him up above everyone.

This is also the way Paul led and how he shook nations. Yes, he wrote powerful letters and spoke for countless hours when he was present with people. Yes, he prayed for the sick. Yes, he loved the person in front of him. But look at his own words about his journey in prayer:

> Without ceasing I mention you always in my prayers.
> —ROMANS 1:9, RSV

> I remember you constantly in my prayers night and day.
> —2 TIMOTHY 1:3, ESV

Therefore I also, after I heard of your faith in the Lord Jesus and your love for all the saints, do not cease to give thanks for you, making mention of you in my prayers.

—Ephesians 1:15–16, nkjv

For this reason we also, since the day we heard it, do not cease to pray for you.

—Colossians 1:9, nkjv

…besides the other things [tribulations], what comes upon me daily: my deep concern for all the churches.

—2 Corinthians 11:28, nkjv

I thank my God upon every remembrance of you, always in every prayer of mine making request for you all with joy.

—Philippians 1:3–4, nkjv

Be constant in prayer.

—Romans 12:12, esv

…praying at all times in the Spirit, with all prayer and supplication. To that end, keep alert with all perseverance, making supplication for all the saints.

—Ephesians 6:18, esv

Pray without ceasing.

—1 Thessalonians 5:17, esv

Prayer for others was at the very core of Paul's life, and it empowered his ministry. It's clear he was convinced of this by his own words.

E. M. Bounds, a nineteenth-century author and clergyman, also attributed Paul's effectiveness in ministry to his journey in prayer:

Paul was a leader by appointment and by universal recognition and acceptance. He had many mighty forces in this ministry. His conversion, so conspicuous and radical, was a great force, a perfect magazine of aggressive and defensive warfare....But these forces were not the divinest energies which brought forth the largest results to his ministry. Paul's course was more distinctly shaped and his career rendered more powerfully successful by prayer than by any other force.[2]

Prayer for others not only releases favor in and around your life; it also softens your heart toward others. It allows God to give you His perspective because you are focusing your mind on Him as you think of others. In this life we will need to forgive others. We will perhaps have to forgive some people seventy times seven. If we are living lives of prayer for others—even those who hurt us—we guard ourselves from the damaging effects of bitterness and anger toward those who have hurt us or those we love. This is transformational. We are called to pray not only for our friends and family and those we have a heart for—we are called to pray even for our enemies.

I want you to have crazy favor with God and men. If you will carry others in your prayers and pray God's dreams into the earth, God will be with you in a unique way. He is looking for friends to share His heart with. It might be your city or your church; it might be Gen Z; it might be unborn babies; it might be a people group. But go on the prayer journey with Him, and you will be surprised by the favor of God that will surround your life and the doors He will open for you.

Anything is possible if you will pray without giving up, especially when you are walking this out with a community of believers. I will repeat that: *anything is possible.* Nothing has to stay the way it is.

THE PASSION OF HANNAH

In the Book of 1 Samuel we meet a woman named Hannah, who earnestly prayed for a son because she was barren. One day she went to the temple to pray, and she was praying so passionately for a son that her lips were moving but no words were coming out. The high priest, Eli, thought she was drunk! But God responded to Hannah's prayers. And He didn't just give her a son—He gave her the greatest prophet of her entire generation. His name was Samuel. Was your last prayer as passionate?

I think right now God is giving many people a passion to pray for Gen Z like Hannah prayed for a son. I am on many prayer lists, and I've noticed that these lists often focus on specific social or political issues. These are important things to pray about because they affect people and nations. But I find myself asking, "Where are those who will cry out like Hannah did and pray for our sons and daughters?"

The statistics are shocking—so many young people are leaving the church. I firmly believe it is possible to win certain cultural wars yet lose a generation. But I believe God is about to take a generation that seems to be more disconnected from Him than ever and use them to bring one of the greatest expressions of His kingdom and love.

God is releasing a message that won't focus primarily on politics or moralism; it will put all the attention on the real Jesus. It will proclaim His

- preexistence—that He lived with the Father before creation,

- incarnation—when God became human and walked the earth,

- life and teaching,

- sacrifice on the cross,

- resurrection,

- ascension—when Jesus returned to heaven and what that means and represents,

- intercession for us now, and

- soon return.

Who Jesus is will captivate hearts. Isaiah says, "In that day the Branch of the LORD [Jesus] will be beautiful and glorious" (Isa. 4:2). The Holy Spirit is going to work overtime to make Jesus known as beautiful in the earth, and this message is going to arrest people's hearts. It's not a new message, but God wants to raise up a new generation to help proclaim it.

That's why people young and old must rise up with the prayer, "We want sons and daughters, and we are going to lift our voices until something supernatural happens in Gen Z." A great awakening is coming to this generation, and God is asking if yours will be one of the voices that bring resurrection. Will you be a part of a resurrection prayer movement? Will you call people to life? Yes, this is a call to get a bit uncomfortable, but it is the best kind of discomfort.

My mom prayed for her dad for decades. Her father was abusive and didn't know Jesus. One year, when he was in his sixties, he announced to our family that he had become a Jesus follower. This had seemed utterly impossible. During that very season, many others in my mom's family began to return to Jesus, leaving alcoholism and various kinds of immorality behind them.

I'll never forget a Thanksgiving dinner with my family. In previous years many of those present were not following Jesus or had wandered from Him. This year was totally different. Revival broke out during our Thanksgiving dinner because my mom and a few other women in our family had been praying for decades. It was the strangest experience I've ever had in an extended family gathering. People were being touched by God everywhere. A chair was set in the middle of the room, and my relatives were receiving prayer one by one. My grandfather got baptized too. Anything is possible when you raise your voice in prayer and refuse to relent.

OPENING DOORS WITH YOUR VOICE

Paul wrote in his letter to the Colossians, "And pray for us, too, that God may open a door for our message, so that we may proclaim the mystery of Christ, for which I am in chains" (Col. 4:3). You can open spiritual doors with your voice. How? You pray what is in heaven down to earth. In fact, within an environment of prayer and worship, church communities can experience an open heaven (Isa. 64:1; John 1:51) that releases awakening, healing, miracles, and other expressions of God's glory and power.

God wants to release so much through our prayers and worship. Our intercession—our spiritual defiance—opens doors for people to hear God's Word. I mean really hear with more than their ears. In the eighteenth century there was a great American missionary named David Brainerd who was focused on the First Nations people coming to know Jesus. He was so passionate about seeing this that he wrote in his journals, "God enabled me so to agonize in prayer, that I was quite wet with sweat, though in the shade, and the cool wind. My soul was drawn out very much for the world; for multitudes of souls."[3]

Brainerd faced many challenges, including his own poor health and the difficulties of not speaking the language and having to use an interpreter. But what happened?

According to his own journals, whole groups would come under such conviction while he spoke that they actually would begin to cry out to God. It was as if entire groups of people would be struck to the core. When we pray for God to open a door for His Word, there is no force on earth like what can be released.

Will you accept the invitation to step into the spiritual defiance of prayer?

Chapter 12

CREATING A FAMILY CULTURE

He who loves his dream of a community more than the Christian community itself becomes a destroyer of the latter, even though his personal intentions may be ever so honest and earnest and sacrificial.

—DEITRICH BONHOEFFER, *LIFE TOGETHER*

IN OUR JOURNEY over the last few years to disciple the nation and the next generation in hosting Jesus' presence on campuses and in cities, God's resolute commitment to relational authenticity and the culture of family has become abundantly clear. I believe God is going to change the understanding and expression of Christianity over the whole earth in one generation, as IHOP-KC founder Mike Bickle says.[1] At the core of that change will be believers who increasingly step into their identities as worshippers and thus orient their whole lives around hosting the presence of God. However, just embracing a lifestyle of worship and prayer, albeit central, is actually not enough.

God's value for championing and serving others in the context of real friendship is surprising in its intensity. Many leaders can slip into creating a culture that is more oriented around building a ministry than a family, but God's vision is family. Even those of us who are passionate about family can slip into this.

As I said earlier, the most significant takeaway from our epic gathering on the National Mall was not the fact that tens of thousands of people attended. It was the lasting sense of connection and family that emerged across states and regions as a result of those four days together in DC. This is clearly what Jesus is moving His people toward.

Said another way, God is shifting us away from making large events our primary focus. Yes, there are catalytic, sovereign moments that happen as believers converge for large-scale gatherings. And yes, organizations need vision to accomplish the work God has called them to do. Without vision we perish. Clear vision can change the world. But God ultimately is creating a family built on Holy Spirit–empowered friendships.

I am naturally a task-oriented person. I thrive in dreaming big dreams and pursuing audacious initiatives for the sake of the gospel. And I spent a number of years getting an unhealthy sense of identity out of what I was accomplishing. This, I discovered, leads to burnout and rings hollow relatively quickly. We were born for authentic connections with others that are nurtured in a culture of honor and love. The litmus test of our love for God is actually our love for one another.

Only—absolutely only—that which is done for love will remain. This includes love for Jesus and love for others. According to Paul in 1 Corinthians 13, you can go as far as martyrdom and do it for reasons other than love. And when that happens, even that sacrifice becomes worthless.

Oneness, Not Just Unity

I think Jesus' prayer in John 17:20–21 is perhaps the most audacious statement ever made about human relationships. Jesus said:

> My prayer is not for them alone. I pray also for those who will believe in me through their message, that all of them may be one, Father, just as you are in me and I am in you. May they also be in us so that the world may believe that you have sent me.

In this final prayer before Jesus went to the cross, He asked the Father to make us one in the same way the Father and Son are one. This is far beyond unity around a simple task or even agreement on some core values. This is a work of God's power in groups of people that causes us to prefer one another, serve one another, support one another, and feel for one another as we would for ourselves. Oneness is God's goal for us.

Two thousand years ago, when God crashed in on 120 people in that Upper Room in Jerusalem, they were in a level of relationship unlike anything the world had seen. But what's even more compelling is what happened after the Holy Spirit began to live among them with greater power than had ever been witnessed in prior history. The most remarkable outcome was the oneness and love they had for one another. Many have tried to replicate this through various structures and methods. But this kind of love and unity happens only where Jesus is present. Thus, pursuing this culture of mutual love and authentic relationship is key to hosting Jesus' presence.

To use Paul's language, we are being built together into a habitation for God by the Spirit (Eph. 2:22). Jesus dwells in the relationships that are built around Him—He is more present there than at events. I don't know if you caught that, but this means that investing in Jesus-centered relationships is the same as building a habitation for God. Of the many things to invest in, investing in people should be at the top of the list.

SERVANTS OF ALL

One of the most basic human tendencies, even in church and ministry environments, is to serve and help others only if there's some kind of payoff. However, Jesus served us out of love, even to the point of death. There is a measure of God's presence and authority that we will not begin to receive until we fundamentally repent of the mindset that seeks to leverage others more than to love and serve them. It's time to be done with leveraging our relationships. People feel it. It's not a secret to anyone. When we're relating to someone just because of what he or she can do for us, it becomes a stench. But the reality is that we have become so accustomed to the smell, we barely notice it anymore.

This is why Jesus said in John 17:21 that when we are one, the world will then believe He was sent from the Father. It's not just when we have more healings or miracles or better communication tools for spreading the gospel. Rather, when our love for one another begins to look increasingly like the love of God, that's what will cause the world around us to pause, take note, and realize something otherworldly is going on with those Jesus people.

They will see Jesus as He is. I am proposing a culture shift. May we no longer see others primarily as resources or tools to accomplish something; let us see them as Jesus sees them—as beloved. It is time to get free from the spirit that seeks to control and find freedom in meekness.

When we discover our identities in Jesus, we are free to love one another, and we stop using people and harming our relationships. It is as the Dutch theologian Henri J. Nouwen wrote:

> There is much mental suffering in our world. But some of it is suffering for the wrong reason because it is born out of the false expectation that we are called to take each other's loneliness away. When our loneliness drives us away from ourselves into the arms of our companions in life, we are, in fact, driving ourselves into excruciating relationships, tiring friendships and suffocating embraces....No friend or lover, no husband or wife, no community or commune will be able to put to rest our deepest cravings for unity and wholeness. And by burdening others with these divine expectations, of which we ourselves are often only partially aware, we might inhibit the expression of free friendship and love.[2]

The Power of Meekness

Years ago I was a young man filled with ambition and zeal for what I felt Jesus called me to do. I was newly married and was between jobs, so I decided to go into a season of fasting and prayer for God to show me my next steps in ministry. This fast was a big deal in my mind.

I was on day eleven of the fast, and I was exhausted. On top of that, I had heard nothing from God. Nada. Zip.

There was one verse that kept resonating in my heart during all these days of fasting and prayer: "I have seen all the things that are done under the sun; all of them are meaningless, a chasing after the wind" (Eccles. 1:14).

I kept thinking about the line "a chasing after the wind." How could I be chasing after the wind when the things I was pursuing were so soaked in good intentions? I even had the sense that God was speaking to my heart about specific things He called me to do. How could this be a chasing after the wind?

I have since learned that this is a common experience among those who have vision from God. God kills the vision so the vision doesn't kill you. He wants to protect you from yourself so you can ultimately fulfill the vision. I wish someone had filled me in on this principle at that time.

After those eleven days of fasting and prayer, I heard a message on the life of David. David's core values were, first, intimacy with God and, secondarily, serving others within a culture of honor. I realized then that God was not giving me the details for how to accomplish the things He placed in my heart because He wanted me to focus entirely on cultivating intimacy with Him and showing meekness to others. He wanted those two values to be my definition of greatness for the rest of my life.

I remember walking outside on a cold February day, feeling the pain of unanswered questions. I was filled with zeal; I had ideas and even a plan drawn out of what my ministry would look like. Yet God was closing every door. Meetings I set up with key leaders to share the vision were all canceled at the last minute. I knew God was resisting me. This was not the enemy. As I walked alone and communed with Jesus that day, I prayed for the first time what has become my life vision, and I have prayed this thousands of times since: "Jesus, I ask You to let intimacy and meekness define my life."

Meekness is a strange word. In the Sermon on the Mount, Jesus said, "Blessed are the meek, for they will inherit the earth" (Matt. 5:5). When we are meek, we take all of our resources and strength and use them for other people's benefit. We get under others and lift them up. When we are meek, we actually give out of our resources and possibly forgo opportunities for ourselves if it serves others' success. Meek people treat others gently, even in their failings.

Could there be anything more countercultural than this? The systems around us teach us to pursue our own external successes, no matter the cost. Jesus taught us that success is actually in the success of those He placed around us. Our greatness is in helping others be great. Our joy is more in giving than receiving. Having said that, when you are living in meekness toward people, God will promote you supernaturally.

Meekness is like a magnet for favor. God loves to spend time with humble people.

What Jesus was saying in the Sermon on the Mount is that only meek people are going to inherit everything in the age to come. Meek people get the earth. To say it another way, no one who is operating in pride or selfish ambition will have leadership in Jesus' kingdom.

Serving others does not always mean taking a back seat to everything; sometimes it means stepping out in bold leadership. David, for instance, served others and was still regarded as a powerful and influential king. But he was always willing to let

God deal with him in the most profound ways at the heart level so he could function in his assignment. Meekness is something that happens at the heart level. It is a posture toward God that is reflected in our interactions with others.

The Saul Factor

It may sound strange, but I believe one of God's greatest gifts to David was Saul. The one who seemed bent on David's destruction and undoing ultimately prepared him for his place of influence as king of Israel. I say this because David's great enemy was not actually Saul; it was David. God allowed Saul in David's life so David would not become another Saul.

Many times we are frustrated by people who mistreat us. However, even if what they are doing is completely wrong, God allowed them in our lives for our own good—to teach us meekness and humility. This is what David learned, and this is incredibly important for us to learn if we are going to host the presence of Jesus.

The favor that comes with Jesus' blessing and presence is so powerful that without going through the school of meekness, that favor can hurt us. Jesus is set on helping us carry this kind of favor.

Even the presence of God, which is what we desire so deeply, can cause people to get puffed up and confused when God is moving powerfully through them. But because God wants to move powerfully through you, He sends you to the school of meekness as a prerequisite for realizing the God-sized dream of your heart. God wants the measure of your meekness to equal the measure of your calling.

Jesus said the greatest in the kingdom of God are the servants of all (Matt. 23:11). Once you see this, pursuing a culture of meekness will become a primary prayer focus and lifestyle choice. God does want to promote you. Impacting those around you is not a bad desire. However, God promotes only those who are committed to using their power, however much or little, to love and serve other people, even to their own detriment at times.

The reality is this: Saul could not steal David's destiny in God, and no one can steal your destiny. The fear of loss keeps people in pride because they are buying into the lie that the Sauls of their lives can actually steal what God wants to give them. Sometimes in a short-term way that can happen, but at the core of the life of meekness is trust that God will always lift up the humble and defend the persecuted.

When you know that no Saul can steal your destiny, then you can be free to love and forgive people from the heart. That is not to say people will never hurt us or that we should put ourselves in positions to be hurt by others. It is simply to say we will get hurt sometimes, and our responses matter eternally.

As always, Jesus has the answer. Here is how we must respond to the Sauls of our lives:

> I say to you, love your enemies, bless those who curse you, do good to those who hate you, and pray for those who spitefully use you and persecute you, that you may be sons of your Father in heaven; for He makes His sun rise on the evil and on the good, and sends rain on the just and on the unjust.
> —MATTHEW 5:44–45, NKJV

God will vindicate you, but I will tell you what is more important than that. It is what happens in your heart as you bless those who hate you. God wants to give you a free heart filled with love, which is the greatest reward of embracing a posture of forgiveness and mercy.

Your meekness will be tested many times and in many ways, but God is at work in these tests. One of the greatest challenges is to keep quiet and not defend yourself when someone has hurt you or spoken falsely of you. Not defending ourselves and instead trusting God to be our defense not only sets the other person free since we are no longer in an adversarial relationship with them; it moves us into the great supernatural life God has invited us to be part of.

One of my favorite verses about David is 2 Samuel 5:12: "Then David knew that the LORD had established him as king over Israel and had exalted his kingdom for the sake of his people Israel." This is right after David finally became king of all of Israel after about a fifteen-year journey. Living in the promise looked impossible. David had multiple opportunities to take the kingdom from Saul by force, but he chose to honor Saul as king and trust God to give him the kingdom as He had said.

So when David became king, he knew God had done it. When you get a position by manipulation, you will live in constant insecurity, just as Saul did. You will live in fear and likely lose what you gained in your own strength. David knew God established him as king. He was put in that position to fulfill his assignment for the sake of others.

When God establishes you, then you can be confident. There is nothing about humility that would cause us to be timid or insecure in what God has called us to do and be. David knew God had established him, and he boldly stepped into the role of king but only after God had generously prepared him.

Sometimes it will seem as though God has killed the vision when He allows circumstances that make it look impossible for the dream to become a reality. But He is the God of resurrection. He will do it.

You can trust God for your destiny, and you can dream big dreams, but let your biggest dream be intimacy with God and meekness toward others. Whether or not you are well-known in the world, you will be great in heaven if you pursue these things with your whole heart.

Sometimes we don't just fear that someone will steal our

destinies by mistreatment but that someone else's promotion could hinder us. No one else's promotion will ultimately steal your destiny if you can learn to celebrate others' victories from the heart. This is a lesson you must learn to be a leader in the move of God. No one can steal your destiny. No one is truly a threat to you. God will make a way for you if you give yourself to meekness.

BUILDING BRIDGES

Most moms want to have everyone at the table before they start a holiday meal. I am convinced that God is the same way.

I am convinced that many of the oppressed people groups of the world are going to be primary leaders in the move of God that is coming. I don't believe most people actively hate others based on their ethnicity, but I believe God is calling us to be on the front lines in dealing with the effects of racism on the lives of various people.

In America the Black community has experienced four hundred years of oppression, and the effects of this remain tangible even today. John 17 begs for us to have an ear for those who have experienced suffering, oppression, and racism; to really listen; to give our hearts to building bridges that are more than talking points.

Let us all join in this bridge-building and injustice-smashing movement to heal racial wounds in our cities and nations. This should start with the church. Jesus has given us the ministry of reconciliation, and I don't believe we will receive the fullness of what God wants to do until we are all at the table together in an authentic way.

EMPOWERING THE NEXT GENERATION

If we are going to allow God to do everything He wants, we need to create space for a truly grassroots movement of lovers of God to step into what God has called them to do. One generation is never more important than another, but what is coming is going to require current leaders to give emerging leaders a place at the table right in the middle of the move of God.

God is about family and giving people a sense of belonging. But let's be real here. Getting out of the way and releasing people who are just finding their voices can be downright messy. In our church culture we want professionals. I am in no way suggesting ministry should be sloppy or without direction. But the need for control can keep a move of God stopped up.

Jesus sent out His twelve leaders in Luke 9. He empowered them to be on His team. Yet in that same chapter, the disciples argued right in front of Jesus about which of them was the greatest, and that argument went on for months. Then they told a man to stop casting out a demon because he was not part of their group. And as if that wasn't enough, John and James asked Jesus if He wanted them to call down fire on the Samaritan village that rejected them. This is all in the same chapter—all in the time frame of Jesus releasing them. Jesus corrected each of these mistakes, but He didn't give up on them. Instead He sent out seventy-two more people who had spent even less time with Him (Luke 10:1).

The whole purpose of church leadership, according to Ephesians 4:11–12, is to equip the saints for the work of ministry. That means releasing people to find their voices, even if the process is a bit messy.

What God wants to do is going to take everyone working in collaboration. So if you are part of a younger generation, reach out to spiritual fathers and mothers. You are going to need them to help you navigate what is coming, because you are still growing in wisdom. If you are part of an older generation, spend time with the next generation and be intentional about building relationships with them because no generation can do this alone. We need one another.

THE DREAM STARTS NOW

I believe God is knitting people together who have a shared value for hosting Jesus' presence and long to serve a move of God right now. We are finding one another. This dream of God is too big for any of us to do alone. We need one another. In some ways, I have grown to believe this is the primary assignment God has given me. Our relationships within the community of believers are an end in and of themselves. They are not just the means to accomplish a goal.

I had a dream a number of years ago, and in it I saw a map of the East Coast of the United States. I saw challenging times coming, and in the dream I called my good friend Benjamin Atkinson and said, "We need to combine our houses of prayer to go day and night so that lives will be spared and revival will come."

A couple of months later we decided to gather about thirty different leaders who were pursuing prayer and worship in Virginia to meet and get to know one another. This sounds so simple. But this is God's way.

The night before the first gathering, which we called 24/7 Virginia, God woke Benjamin up and said, "David's dream starts now."

What happened is that we began to collaborate. People began even moving from one city to another. Through that gathering, we learned that God wanted us connected and that His plan for Virginia would only unfold through our relationships. We didn't realize at the time that God was going to allow us to see something similar unfold across the nation. As I mentioned earlier, the Awaken the Dawn leadership network was a national expression of what God began in our state. Could we serve one another, dream with one another, and collaborate without a controlling spirit? Could we be one as Jesus and the Father are one?

Let's make it our aim to "outdo one another in showing honor" (Rom. 12:10, ESV). Let's dream big. Let's dream of meekness filling our lives and spheres.

PART IV

WHERE DO WE GO FROM HERE?

Chapter 13

THE SILVER BULLET

Is this not the fast that I have chosen: to loose the bonds of wickedness, to undo the heavy burdens, to let the oppressed go free, and that you break every yoke? Is it not to share your bread with the hungry, and that you bring to your house the poor who are cast out; when you see the naked, that you cover him, and not hide yourself from your own flesh? Then your light shall break forth like the morning, your healing shall spring forth speedily.

—ISAIAH 58:6–8, NKJV

W HEN IT COMES to the topic of hosting Jesus' presence in our cities and regions, I am increasingly convinced that there is a marriage in God's heart between worship and prayer and missions and gospel proclamation. In fact I think it's increasingly hard to tell where one stops and the other starts. Naturally speaking, we are prone to isolate these things. We think prayer people and evangelism people can live in two different worlds. But what God has joined together, let no one separate.

This is particularly relevant as we are discussing David's tent. As you might recall, David's tent refers to the 24/7 worship David established in a literal tent in Jerusalem that housed God's presence in the form of the ark of the covenant. The worship continued nonstop for more than thirty years with thousands of musicians participating, and it brought a manifestation of God's presence that changed history.

In Acts 15:16–17 God said He will rebuild David's tabernacle: "Its ruins I will rebuild, and I will restore it, that the rest of mankind may seek the Lord, even all the Gentiles who bear my name, says the Lord, who does these things." Notice the passage says the purpose of David's tabernacle being restored is so "the rest of mankind may seek the Lord."

In other words, David's tent is missional. Its actual purpose is not just to create a resting place for God's presence but also to be an environment where people who are far from God can seek and find Him. That's the key thing. The invitation is to seek and find Jesus—not a philosophical system, code of morality, or even church organization, but Jesus' personal presence. As we build our communities around Jesus' presence, we are actually setting the table for people who are far from God to come in and feast on Him.

Jesus is setting a table. David's tent is about creating a table for people who are far from God, a place of belonging.

A DIVINE APPOINTMENT

Another couple of my heroes are Brian and Christy Brennt. They are the founders and leaders of the Circuit Riders, based in Orange County in Southern California. The Circuit Riders are raising up an army of young leaders who are taking the gospel to university campuses and everywhere in between. They lead one of the most joyful communities that I know of.

In 2019 I was in Southern California for an Awaken the Dawn event but wanted to catch up with Brian and Christy, especially since Christy had just been healed of chronic Lyme's disease, which had her largely bedridden for over thirty years. I was so excited to hear the story. She was healed at The Send, a large stadium gathering in Orlando, Florida, in February of 2019. God had shown her years ago that she would be healed, and the promise had finally been fulfilled. Now for the first time in her adult life, Christy was able to function normally.

Excited to hear the whole story, I jumped in my rental car and set out to drive from San Diego to Orange County. As the stunning scenery of the California coastline rolled by on my left, I called my wife.

"Where are you going?" she asked.

"I am going to spend some time with Brian and Christy Brennt," I replied without much thought.

"Who?" Ashley seemed especially interested.

"You know, Brian Brennt."

Ashley didn't yet know Brian and Christy personally.

"That's the Brian I told you about!" Ashley said. "Maybe now's the time he has that word for you."

Then I remembered.

A couple of years earlier Ashley came to me and said that while she was praying earlier in the day, God had spoken to her that Brian Brennt was going to have a word for me that was really important. The thing about this is that when the Holy Spirit spoke this to Ashley, she didn't even know who Brian Brennt was. She'd heard his name while on a prayer walk and had no idea Brian Brennt was someone I actually knew.

"Maybe connecting with the Brennts is more important than I realized," I thought. So we prayed that God would speak and do whatever He wanted through the meeting.

The Brennts' garage, where so much worship has gone forth, is more of a living room. It's where legends have gathered and many dreams have been birthed, and I learned as we talked that day that one of the things Jesus had shown Christy in a powerful encounter was a mobile tent movement. It was like the tent where Billy Graham started preaching in Los Angeles many decades ago but included healing and amazing miracles. At that time, we had started hosting tent gatherings from coast to coast in America. Christy's vision included more than what we were doing, but I couldn't help but notice the overlap. Could this be part of the word from Brian Brennt?

As we sat in the Brennts' garage, I looked up, and hanging on the wall was a handwritten poster with a word from Jill Austin that someone had recently shared with me as well. The word spoke of mobile tents traveling across our nation like mobile houses of prayer that would be filled with God's glory.

I had this thought that day in their garage, and I said it out loud: "What if the gospel tents and the worship tents are converging together? *The tents are like a silver bullet to see awakening in America.*"

Later that evening, I was scheduled to speak at our Awaken the Dawn gathering in San Diego. I wrote in my notes what I had said to Brian and Christy: the tents are a silver bullet for awakening in America. I was pondering how day-and-night worship could converge with gospel proclamation and healing in public. I was struck by how tents could allow this in such a unique way and actually take Jesus' presence and the gospel to public places all over the nation.

A silver bullet is a metaphor that refers to a seemingly "magical" solution to a complex problem. It speaks of the catalytic tool to accomplish something important. It would be just like the foolishness of God to call people out of million-dollar buildings and into tents and from there to pour out the Holy Spirit on campuses and cities. What an intriguing thought. I couldn't stop mulling over the idea of thousands of tents flooding America, giving voice to thousands of musicians and messengers and filling America with the gospel.

Right before I stood up to speak at the event in San Diego, a woman named Jessie, whom I'd just met, approached me and pulled a silver bullet out of her bag—an actual bullet made of real silver. She handed it to me and said, "The Holy Spirit told me to bring this and give it to you tonight." On the very day of my conversation with Brian and Christy, this woman felt led to give me a silver bullet. I stood amazed at God's timing.

I had my notes right there in front of me. I was going to stand up that night and say the tents are a silver bullet for an awakening in our nation and the world. She could not have known that. I felt this must be a confirmation of my conversation earlier in the day—not just a confirmation of God wanting to use the tool of tents but in a broader sense of the convergence between gospel proclamation, compassion, day-and-night worship, and the presence of God. What kinds of breakthroughs would take place on campuses and in cities if day-and-night worship and prayer, acts of compassion, and gospel proclamation were flooding the streets?

I believe tents are a silver bullet for spiritual awakening for three reasons.

First, tents get us outside our normal infrastructure and the four walls of our usual church environments and in so doing, bring diverse people together. God is more interested in building a family than organizations. We have discovered that because these tent gatherings are in neutral locations, people tend to come together from different church communities, ethnicities, organizations, and movements. They come together around Jesus' presence and the gospel. Gathering in tents has built bridges and connected hearts in ways that are surprising even to our team.

Second, tents facilitate day-and-night worship and prayer just as David's tent did three thousand years ago. There's something about setting up a centralized location for people to gather and worship around-the-clock. Where two or three are gathered in Jesus' name, He's actually there (Matt. 18:20). So it's much less about the tents than it is about Jesus being in the middle of our cities.

Third, tents are in public for a reason—so the good news of Christ can be proclaimed to our campuses, cities, and nations. I have often said that if all we are trying to do is lead prayer meetings, we would host them inside. We have plenty of buildings that can be used for that completely valid purpose. The idea of gathering in tents, as Bob Jones told me years ago, is for the express purpose of bringing prayer and worship to public, outdoor spaces so we can engage the broader community with the gospel. This means the primary sound coming from public tent gatherings should be the gospel.

I frequently encourage those who are part of our movement to remember that we are outdoors and in public for a reason. Remember, on the day of Pentecost after the Holy Spirit fell in the Upper Room, Peter had to go out in front of the crowd that had gathered and actually proclaim Jesus. He couldn't just stay inside. What happens in the prayer room is vitally important, but it's not meant to stay there. The gospel also needs to be proclaimed in word, deed, and song.

Speaking of what happens in the prayer room, there may be some things that make a lot of sense to do in a prayer room, but they don't make nearly as much sense when you're in public. There are things you do in your bedroom that most certainly would not be appropriate on your front porch. So while this movement is definitely about intimacy and fellowship with God, we need to be aware that we're there to serve others. Specifically we're there to serve people as they discover and encounter Jesus as He really is.

A Game Changer

Something else came up through that conversation with Brian and Christy that has proven to be a game changer.

"What if you brought the tents to the places where stadium gatherings were going to happen?" Brian said.

This struck my heart. What if whenever there is a massive stadium gathering, which are surely coming as a great awakening begins to break out, there are tent gatherings for extended periods leading up to the stadium event in that city? What if there was already an open heaven over the city when the stadium event began because of the worship and prayer that had been flooding the atmosphere? What if people were already coming together across diverse racial and denominational backgrounds? What if healing and salvation were already breaking out? In a stadium only a few people can realistically be on the stage. But with tents everywhere, thousands of Billy Grahams could be raising their voices and loving their cities all at the same time.

At the very moment I was pondering this idea, Brian told me The Send was planning an event at Arrowhead Stadium in Kansas City, Missouri. Kansas City is deeply meaningful to me because of the day-and-night prayer that has risen from there through the International House of Prayer. A couple of days after this significant meeting with Brian, Lou Engle called me. There was no mistaking his scruffy voice on the other line.

"I'm praying for you today," he said. "Have you ever thought of bringing the tents to the places where the stadiums are happening?"

I was surprised by his question. "Did you talk to Brian Brennt?" I asked.

You would think after all the times the Lord had done things like this, I'd be used to it. But it never gets old. I was still taken aback that Lou was expressing the same idea Brian had just shared days earlier. I felt like I was being carried along, getting to take part in something I had no control over. Someone else was clearly writing this story.

"No," Lou answered. "Why?"

I told Lou about my recent meeting with Brian and Christy Brennt. And after talking with Lou, I was more than seriously considering moving toward this collaboration between tent and stadium gatherings. Soon after these conversations, we took a team of about fifty leaders out to the Kansas City area to Harry Truman's old farm, which is now owned by the International House of Prayer, and prayed and worshipped for thirty hours on site. There God confirmed the partnership with The Send in our hearts.

As much as we are called to follow God's leading as individuals and unique movements, something is coming that requires all of us to link arms and hearts while saying yes. As hundreds of tents have filled campuses and cities over the last few years, it's clear the silver bullet is already in motion. On one campus a young man was walking by one of our tents. He had written his suicide note that day and was on his way to carry out his tragic, heartbreaking plan. But as he passed by the tent, he heard the music and walked in. Little did he know, this simple decision to walk into a tent would forever change his life.

He later said he was inexplicably drawn to the little tent in the middle of the campus. That night, a group of students surrounded the young man. He felt so valued and loved by God as the students prayed for him. This young man met Jesus while walking in the middle of his university campus. But it took people being present at the right time and in the right place, just praying and worshipping the Lord, to meet him at the point of his need.

On another campus there was a Jewish student on his way to his religious group to celebrate the Feast of Tabernacles with them. He also was drawn in by the music and stumbled into the tent. He was intrigued by the fact that the gathering was happening during the Feast of Tabernacles and ended up in a brilliant conversation about Jesus. His heart was quickened, and he met his Messiah that night.

I think God is asking us to get dirty with Him. We ask Him all the time to come to our events, but I think He is asking who will go out to where He is calling. He is asking us to go out where He longs to show Himself among those who would never set foot in our churches. The coming awakening is about more than individual ministries and callings. It's about being part of the story Jesus is writing in the earth.

Chapter 14

THE COMING FESTIVAL

Joy is the serious business of Heaven.

—C. S. LEWIS, *LETTERS TO MALCOLM*

I T IS ONE thing to have dreams or visions about something; it is an even more powerful thing to know that what you dream of is prophesied in the Scriptures. I believe the Bible speaks of a movement of joyful gatherings of worship that is key to God's plan.

In chapter 10 I referenced Isaiah chapters 24 and 42. Both of these prophetic passages speak of a joyful musical movement that's literally going to fill the earth. But they also speak of public places—mountaintops, coastlands, and cities—*lifting their voices.* This is like a global festival of glory—a festival around Jesus' presence.

FESTIVAL LIFESTYLE

I am gripped right now as we are watching the festival culture explode globally among the youth of the world. It is hitting a level that the world has rarely seen.

Why do people go to festivals like Coachella or Bonnaroo or Tomorrowland, which is billed as "the world's largest dance music festival"?[1] People attend because they are looking for community and belonging, and they're finding it in these environments. They go because there is music and consequently spiritual experiences (which are often enhanced by drug use). And they go because there's a sense of mission and justice, as there is usually a cause being championed.

These three concepts belong to Jesus. He is calling for a

global movement that builds true community and belonging, invites people to encounter Him, and gives expression to His mission and justice. What the world offers are really only counterfeits of what God is doing. Jesus is the originator of these concepts.

Whenever I see an image of one of these massive festivals, I can't help but think about what God has in His heart. We have sometimes used the phrase *festival lifestyle* because, though there is certainly no way to live in event mode all the time nor would we even want to, God is inviting Christian communities into a culture of celebration around His presence. Having said that, I think there are massive gatherings coming that carry this culture of unspeakable joy, and this is part of how God is going to set the table for many to come into the family of God. I believe Isaiah saw this. God is bringing people into a place of belonging.

THE GREAT *HALAL*

If you've spent much time in church, you've probably said and sung the word *hallelujah* many times. This Hebrew word comes from *halal*, which means praise. *Hallelujah* means praise the Lord. But the word *halal* is very interesting. According to Strong's concordance, it means "to boast; and thus to be (clamorously) foolish; to rave…(sing, be worthy of) praise."[2] So a halal celebration is wild at times, just like many popular music festivals.

There is a great halal coming. There will be songs and music and community, and it will be holy and will fill cultures with God's presence. I believe this is in God's blueprint for our church communities.

History actually culminates in the greatest feast ever in Jesus' presence. It's called the marriage supper of the Lamb. If you know Jesus, you will be in attendance. This is your destination.

It would only make sense that there would be down payments of that across the world. Imagine this scene in the future. The marriage supper of the Lamb is when we all see Jesus face to face. There has been no festival, no celebration that can compare to that future moment.

John described it in the Book of Revelation:

> Then I heard what sounded like a great multitude, like the roar of rushing waters and like loud peals of thunder, shouting: "Hallelujah! For our Lord God Almighty reigns. Let us rejoice and be glad and give him glory! For the wedding of the Lamb has come, and his bride has made herself ready. Fine linen, bright and clean, was given her to wear." (Fine linen represents the righteous acts of God's holy people.) Then the angel said to me, "Write this: Blessed are those who are invited to the wedding supper of the Lamb!"
>
> —REVELATION 19:6–9

This passage says *our voices* are going to thunder in celebration. This is not hype or simple frivolity. It is much deeper than that. And there are amazing down payments on this very thing coming to a city near you.

I love the verse in Isaiah 56 where God says He will make us joyful in His house of prayer (Isa. 56:7). God says, like it or not, if you will embrace the prayer lifestyle with others, you will become joyful. This extreme joy is found in Jesus' presence and nowhere else. I believe the joy of the Lord in our cities is about to confront everything else, including all the arguments against Jesus. How do you argue with someone who is filled with a joy that is actually unspeakable and full of glory (1 Pet. 1:8)?

This is why the tents are part of the story. They are a witness to the pleasures forever that are found in Jesus.

Move Into the New

This is a time of great uncertainty, but I am convinced it is one of the best times to be alive and following Jesus. Jesus does not go backward, only forward, and He is moving. The key is for us to be more connected to Him than even to the work itself. So much has already happened in this journey with Awaken the Dawn and in our lives, but I want to follow the Lamb in every season.

That is why I knew I needed to seek Him personally when the COVID-19 pandemic hit in 2020. It proved to be a turning point.

Right before I left for a week of prayer and fasting, my wife and I had almost identical dreams within a very short time frame. We had recently moved into a new house, and in both of our dreams we were in our old house. In our dreams we defaulted to going to sleep in our old bedroom at the old house. In both dreams we woke up and realized the house we fell asleep in was no longer our house.

We shouldn't have been sleeping in a house that was no longer ours. We were overwhelmed with embarrassment that we had trespassed without thinking. We needed to be in our new house and not return to what was. That house may have been ours in the past, but we had a new house now. It was time to move on to the new.

Here is what God was showing us: we cannot default to what worked in the last season. God is doing a new thing, and we are in a new season. Do you perceive it? The only way to move forward is to be more attuned to Jesus and His voice than to the environment around us. We cannot judge this season by the headlines or our experiences. There is more going on than meets the eye. Much more.

RESTORING CITIES

Recently I was in Chicago alone to pray. As I parked in the city, I heard on the news that two people had just been shot in the exact area where I was just fifteen minutes before I arrived. Although I was obviously close to what had become a dangerous situation, all I could think about was how much those two people mattered to God. I can't explain what happened, but I was suddenly overwhelmed by God's heart for the cities of America and the nations.

I believe God's eyes are on our cities, and where we see desolation, He wants to bring healing. While in Chicago I realized it is time to pull out the stops and become even more focused and determined to reach the nation's cities. At the exact time I was experiencing this, a friend texted me that the Holy Spirit stirred her to tell me that worship and prayer within our cities is the key to a great awakening.

I immediately bore witness to what she was saying. The great revivals in the Book of Acts were all based in urban centers. And Jesus' letters in the Book of Revelation were written to churches in urban centers. A movement that touches cities is coming again, and I am daring to believe that these public expressions of worship and the gospel are a part of it. This movement is about far more than gatherings in tents or stadiums. It is about Christian communities learning to host the presence of Jesus, even in the most resistant urban centers in the world. Even where things look so challenging, I believe there is opportunity.

It's like what Isaiah saw many years ago: "They will renew the ruined cities that have been devastated for generations" (Isa. 61:4).

What was God asking us to do?

Recently we felt led to ask God for a massive tent that we could own and use to host gatherings in cities and on college campuses. This seemed like yet another step of faith. God provided (of course). We were just graciously given a massive tent that could fit thousands of people for Awaken the Dawn to take to campuses and cities. We are calling it America's Awakening Tent.

Our goal is not to enter a region like rock stars. This massive tent is a resource for church communities, campuses, and cities. Our goal is to support what God is already doing in cities and helping local groups do even more than they planned. I believe God is going to take this movement of prayer and worship in tents to the next level.

We are not just about mobilizing people to host events. Our vision is to empower communities of believers to host Jesus together and bring incredible transformation as a result. To be clear, an event alone can't restore a city. That is why we are laboring to serve the Christian communities of a region, invest in them, and support what they are doing the best we can so it brings lasting fruit through the power of the Holy Spirit.

As believers joining together for these new Jesus festivals, we will see widespread salvation, baptisms, and healings in both sober and joyful times in the middle of cities and on college campuses. You see, our endgame is to host more than events; it's to host a movement that transforms the culture around us.

Chapter 15

JESUS IS NOT AN AMERICAN

And [Jesus] said to them, "The harvest is plentiful, but
the laborers are few. Therefore pray earnestly to the Lord
of the harvest to send out laborers into his harvest."

—LUKE 10:2, ESV

I LOVE AMERICA. I think the American experiment is one
of the greatest accomplishments in history. God's heart
is freedom and justice for all, and I believe His purposes for
America are profound, and many have yet to be fulfilled. I love
praying for and serving America. This is my nation, and I have
what I hope is a healthy sense of pride in it despite its flaws.

Having said that, as we are laboring for God's will to be done
and God's kingdom to come, we have to recognize that Jesus is
not American. Jesus is thinking about people groups most of us
never pause to consider.

I signed up for the lifestyle of prayer and to labor for the
movement I have been describing in this book because I discovered what David understood in Psalm 27:4. I loved Jesus' presence, and I wanted more of it. But the amazing thing about
signing up for this lifestyle of worship, prayer, and gospel proclamation is that as we begin to touch God's heart, we discover
that He's thinking about things we don't even care about at
times.

Here is Jesus' endgame:

> And this gospel of the kingdom will be preached in the
> whole world as a testimony to all nations, and then the
> end will come.
>
> —MATTHEW 24:14

So the prayer movement, the missions movement, the church planting movement, and the worship movement are all about the completion of Jesus' commission to make disciples everywhere (Matt. 28:19–20). I believe this Great Commission is like a plumb line. God wants to reorient our thinking away from our personal well-being and around Jesus' ultimate aim, which is that there be a witness to the gospel among every people group on the earth. Jesus will not come back until everyone hears.

As we are laboring for great awakening, we have to understand that it won't be limited to our nation; it will reach the nations of the earth, including the places most hostile to the gospel. God's dream for awakening may be bigger and more challenging than you think. What if God wants to send your son or daughter to places where martyrdom is common? What if God wants to take your church's best and brightest and plant them in these environments? What if God wants to send you? Will you say yes? Will you keep praying for revival if this is where it leads?

God wants us to dream with Him and embrace His vision for souls. You may be praying for a few hundred people to get saved in your community when He wants to bring in tens of thousands. Don't limit what God wants to do because His dream is bigger than yours. As the old saying goes, where God guides, He provides.

When David wanted to build the temple for God thousands of years ago, God would not let him do it and instead gave the task to his son Solomon. But because David was a man after God's own heart and his desire to build God's house was so dear to God, the Lord committed to build David's house forever. When you are aligned with God's heart, you step into a flow of provision. So yes, God wants to move on college campuses and in our cities. But Jesus wants to give us a vision for people groups who don't even know His name. As we focus on His desire (building His house), He will take care of our houses.

THAT ALL MAY HEAR

There are over seven thousand unreached people groups in the world.[1] If God is going to move in our nation, He's going to send people to those groups. You can bank on that.

In fact you see this pattern in the Book of Acts. Paul was launched into ministry from a worshipping, praying, fasting community. It was in that environment, in the church at Antioch in Acts 13, that he was finally sent out on the mission that Jesus had given him years earlier.

Jesus said in Matthew 9:37–38: "The harvest is plentiful but the workers are few. Ask the Lord of the harvest, therefore, to send out workers into his harvest field." The Greek word translated "send" in this passage is *ekballō*. It means "to cast out, drive out, to send out, with notion of violence."[2] There is coming to a city near you a great thrusting forth of laborers to the unreached people groups of the world. You cannot host Jesus' presence and remain detached from this vision, because He is thinking about it.

In America we often say that we are believing God for a third Great Awakening, but what about the places that never had their first great awakening?

We have sent quite a number of people out on new assignments over the years, but I want to mention two specifically.

One of my closest friends and a true sister was launched out of our local Awaken the Dawn base to the Middle East. We will call her Elaine. Launching Elaine out into her call was an extremely painful thing since she was a close friend and an integral part of our leadership team. Though painful, this launching was also a glorious one.

I had been in full-time ministry with Elaine on different

teams for twenty-three years. I didn't want her to go to the Middle East. However, we had been giving ourselves to hosting Jesus' presence with worship and prayer for many years, and one of the things you have to expect when you cultivate an environment like this is that God is going to send some people out. He wants our participation in the story He is writing.

So God began to speak to Elaine over the course of a few years, and we sent her out to live and work in the Middle East. She has seen many people with Muslim backgrounds come to a saving knowledge of Jesus. In the Middle East she worked with a prayer room, a house church network, and an amazing NGO that serves refugees. In retrospect, sending people to the nations is one of the most amazing things I have been a part of, and there is much more to come.

One of my other great friends, Randy Martinez, co-labored with me in ministry for many years. Then God spoke to Randy and a team of people to plant an organization called MAPS Global. Through MAPS Global, Randy and his team are giving themselves to prayer, building a healthy Christian community, and launching laborers all over the world, particularly in the Middle East. This is close to Jesus' heart. God is in the business of birthing new works. Birthing is painful but beautiful. Long-term prayer and worship always lead to new birth.

A Promise to Israel

There was a time early in this journey when I was not focused on anything except wanting more of Jesus and leading a small move of God among youth in our region. Then my brother-in-law had a dream from God. In his dream he walked up to the door of my house and knocked. My friend Elaine opened the door and told him, "There's an angel in the living room with a message for you." So in the dream he went into the living room, and there was an angel. (What kind of crazy life do we live when angels show up in dreams?) The angel said three sentences to him, and the last sentence was, "Tell David Bradshaw to pray for Israel."

At that point in my life, I had never really spent time praying for Israel. I really never even thought about Israel. But this was an interesting dream, so I prayed once or twice for Israel. A couple of weeks later my friend Elaine approached me. She had not heard about my brother-in-law's dream, but she told me she'd had a dream the night before. In it God said three sentences to her. They were the same three sentences the angel spoke to my brother-in-law in his dream, and again the last sentence was, "Tell David Bradshaw to pray for Israel."

What's the big idea here? I believe that to truly embrace the move of God that is coming in the earth, we need to embrace His heart for the Jewish nation. If we love Jesus, we need to love what He loves.

In Romans 9:3 Paul said that he would be cursed and cut off from Christ if it meant the Jewish people would know Jesus (Yeshua) as their Messiah and be saved. Later in the Book of Romans, Paul explained that His people are part of a divine plan that will unfold globally:

> I do not want you to be ignorant of this mystery, brothers and sisters, so that you may not be conceited: Israel has experienced a hardening in part until the full number of the Gentiles has come in, and in this way all Israel will be saved.
>
> —ROMANS 11:25–26

First, the Gentiles (those who are not Jewish) will come to faith while the Jewish people are unwilling to embrace Jesus as their Messiah. That means all the different people groups around the world will hear the gospel and respond to the message of Christ as Matthew 24:14 says. Gentiles are going to come to faith in Jesus by the millions. Many Jewish people also will come to know Yeshua while the Gentiles are coming to Jesus, but many others will remain hardened against believing in Him.

Then something glorious is going to happen. Romans 11:26 tells us all of Israel will be saved. And Paul said when Israel comes to the Messiah en masse, it will be like life from the dead for the whole world (Rom. 11:15).

Here's a statement that might surprise some people: I believe when the Bible talks about Jerusalem, it means Jerusalem. God's not done with the Jewish people. Jewish believers in Jesus wrote almost all of the New Testament, a young Jewish girl gave birth to the Messiah, and ancient Judaism gave us the testimony of what God is like. Make no mistake, God is going to remember His promises to His chosen people. But what's most amazing is that He's going to raise up millions of Gentiles to pray this into being.

The ancient prophet Zechariah said that Jesus' feet will stand on the Mount of Olives (Zech. 14:4). We have to understand that when Jesus returns, He is going to rule the whole world in love. But He will rule the whole world from Jerusalem. This is not one people being favored over another. This is about God's Word, His promises, and His nature.

If God's dream is going to become a reality, we have to realize this is how the story ends—with the salvation of the Jewish people. I pray this vision fills our daydreams and our night dreams.

The Best and Worst of Times

In Matthew 13 Jesus said good and evil will grow to maturity together, and then at the end of the age there will be a harvest. What does that mean? Simply this: things are going to get better and worse at some point in the future.

In other words, before Jesus comes back, there are going to

be amazing expressions of righteousness and love through the church all over the world. I believe cities are going to be transformed. But I also believe there will be great difficulties and for a very short period of time evil will be mature on the earth as well.

This is to say we need to buckle our seatbelts because we are headed into the best and worst of times. But this is not even remotely an invitation for the church to hide out and disengage from the culture. It is the exact opposite of that. We could see whole regions transformed before Jesus comes back, and I believe we will, because the bottom line is this: Something more than revival is coming. Jesus is coming back.

Chapter 16

GOD'S PRESCRIPTION
FOR HEALING

"Yet even now," declares the LORD, "return to me with all your heart, with fasting, with weeping, and with mourning; and rend your hearts and not your garments." Return to the LORD your God, for he is gracious and merciful, slow to anger, and abounding in steadfast love; and he relents over disaster.

—JOEL 2:12–13, ESV

WE ARE FACING some of the most challenging times of our lives. A global pandemic has shaken us to the core. We have seen civil unrest and racism being exposed, we have had challenging elections, and division has heightened all over the world. Many in this generation have lost track of what is right and wrong and can barely tell their right hands from their left. Innocent blood is being shed in the womb and in our streets. In times like these we want to know, How do we respond?

The amazing thing is that God has told us with absolute clarity how to respond in times of shaking, uncertainty, and crisis. He gave us the prescription. It is not a mystery. It is patently clear.

When things are shaking in painful or uncomfortable ways, even those of us who follow Jesus often look for a human remedy. Our immediate, natural response is to lean on our politicians, our money, our churches, or ourselves. God cares about all those things and wants to raise up resources in every sphere to bring about change. But it's essential that we recognize there are things that don't have a remedy outside of Jesus' direct intervention. I am convinced we are in one of those moments.

Jesus loves to step into impossible challenges and show Himself in such a way that only He can get the glory. When we find ourselves in times like the ones we are facing today, we can take heart. God is good and He has given us a clear path to health. It is found in 2 Chronicles 7:14:

> If my people, who are called by my name, will humble themselves and pray and seek my face and turn from their wicked ways, then I will hear from heaven, and I will forgive their sin and will heal their land.

Oftentimes when life is uncertain, people look for some kind of secret, some kind of mystery or conspiracy that will somehow explain what's happening or provide a way out. They are often looking for someone to blame. In all the talking, it's easy to miss the shocking simplicity of what God says to do in uncertain times. It is not complicated. And that is part of the problem. Sometimes it is hard to see what is staring us right in the face. So let's look at this simple and clear prescription from Scripture.

IF MY PEOPLE, WHO ARE CALLED BY MY NAME

Second Chronicles 7:14 was written to Israel, but the principle applies to all Jesus followers. You are the people who are called by His name. You are not like those who do not know Him. You have access to Jesus personally. So you can make a difference in the lives of those around you—in your church, in your city, and on college campuses. Your voice really matters.

This also means that when nations are shaking, God's eyes are on the church first. God's discipline always begins with us because He loves us (1 Pet. 4:17). This is why sin and dysfunction are being exposed in the church. God is perfecting us. This is a process, and it starts with our turning to Him in obedience.

Will Humble Themselves

Humility is not self-deprecation. It is not making yourself feel bad. It's not depression. Humble people are the most joyful of people. To be humble is simply to be in touch with reality. Those who are arrogant, especially in the midst of challenging times, are simply out of touch with the reality of their total dependence on God and need to turn to Jesus with all of their hearts. To be humble is to be aware that there is no human remedy to life's challenges and to set your eyes on Jesus.

And Pray

So then prayer becomes the remedy. If we will pray, mercy will break out in our communities. That sounds overly spiritual when people long for justice, healing, and practical change. But few people have a true understanding of how powerful prayer is. If we will pray, God will intervene—and it will save lives.

As I've mentioned, I live in a town called Fredericksburg, Virginia, just outside of DC. This is where George Washington grew up. George's mother was named Mary Washington, and she was a fiery, praying mom. She was relentless. There's a rock in our town marking the spot where Mary Washington went daily to pray. It's called Meditation Rock. This place was so important to Mary that she asked to be buried there, and that is where her grave is to this day.

Sometimes I've wondered why God raised up Awaken the Dawn in Fredericksburg of all places. As I've pondered that question, I've realized it's likely because of Mary Washington's legacy of prayer. Mary prayed daily for her son and for this fledgling nation during the darkest moments of the American Revolution, and her prayers still matter to God.

George Washington is famously known as the father of the nation, but few of our history books mention his mother's prayers. I believe they were just as significant as what George accomplished. Mary sought God's face in one of the darkest and most challenging times in American history, and her prayers were key not just to the preservation of George's life but also the preservation of thousands of lives and the birthing of the American experiment. Mary understood part of the prescription God gives for uncertain times: to pray.

But I also want to draw your attention to a key found in Joel 2, which is a companion chapter to 2 Chronicles 7. We are told to gather in prayer *with fasting*: "'Even now,' declares the LORD, 'return to me with all your heart, with fasting and weeping and mourning.' Rend your heart and not your garments. Return to the LORD your God, for he is gracious and compassionate, slow to anger and abounding in love, and he relents from sending calamity" (Joel 2:12–13). I believe now is the time for Joel 2 prayer meetings all over the nations. So much spiritual activity happens when we add fasting to our prayers.

AND SEEK MY FACE

The very clear prescription in uncertain times is to seek Jesus' face. The Hebrew word translated "face" in 2 Chronicles 7:14, *pānîm*, is the same word used for *presence*.[1] This paints an important picture:

> In his great work *The Trinity*, Augustine repeatedly cites one particular verse, Psalm 105:4: "Seek his face always." The eminent historian Robert Louis Wilken says of this verse, "More than any other passage in the Bible it captures the spirit of early Christian thinking."[2]

When we talk about the presence of Jesus, we are talking about His face. We are talking about your eyes meeting His eyes. It's personal. It is when God shows Himself to you in a way that causes you to experience His reality personally. This is what God means when He says, "Seek My face." Some will actually have visions of Jesus. Some will not have visions but will experience Jesus' nearness in such personal and real ways that it will change them forever. But the invitation is to seek His face, not just His power.

On people's face you see their emotions. You can see that you have their attention. Eye contact is a big deal in most cultures. When you're looking someone in his eyes, it means he has your undivided attention, you want to hear him, and you have something to say to him. This is what it means to seek God's face. He wants to hear you, and He wants you to hear Him in a way that changes your mindset. "Seek My face" is not simply an abstraction.

This is what compelled David three thousand years ago, and it's what compels us now: there is more. I am convinced that there are things in Jesus I have never known or experienced but that are available to me. There are adventures still yet to be known. The angels around God's throne know this. I think they would say to us, "There is so much more you haven't seen, known, experienced, or encountered."

God is inviting us to seek His actual face. The reality is that you can know Him a million times better than you know Him now. I personally long for this knowledge of Him above everything else in life because there's nothing better.

So in the difficult times we're not seeking a formula or philosophical system but a real, living, breathing person who is the answer to all of our questions.

And Turn From Their Wicked Ways

The first time we ever set up Neil's massive tent here in Fredericksburg, thousands of young people came to worship and encounter Jesus. There was so much joy. But right in the middle of the gathering, something happened that was so unusual I have to mention it here.

My friends Allen Hood and Corey Russell came to join us under the tent as guest speakers. One of our young leaders had an unusual dream a couple of weeks before the event. She dreamed that Allen Hood's son was missing and we were praying for him to be found.

About an hour or so before Allen was going to share under this massive tent, he got a call from his wife. She was at the beach with their kids, and one of their sons was missing. It was exactly what happened in the dream.

We began to pray.

"What do you want to do?" I asked Allen.

He decided to go ahead and speak but keep his phone on him, as he was waiting to hear back from his wife about the whereabouts of his son. As you can imagine, Allen's heart was heavy with emotion as he stood up that day to give his talk.

But there was more going on that day. Allen and Corey had been traveling around our region to visit the Civil War battlefields. There are four battlefields from the American Civil War in the greater Fredericksburg area. In fact there was more bloodshed, brother against brother, in our area than anywhere in America in its entire history. As Allen and Corey were touring the battlefields to spend some time together, Allen found himself in prayer for America. Talk about a disruption to "bro time."

You see, during the Civil War there was a move of God among soldiers. In fact it's the only real identifiable move of God that we know of in the history of our city. All the old churches were packed every night. Many people were encountering God and having amazing experiences with His love as they gave their lives to Jesus. It was absolutely amazing.

The troubling part is that the next day the young men would step onto the battlefield, and many of them lost their lives. In this revival God was showing His love and mercy toward these soldiers so they would not die and spend eternity separated from Him. As Allen and Corey toured the battlefields, they were struck by the realization that there are two kinds of spiritual awakening.

One kind prepares people so they are not separated from God in the midst of crisis. If you look at the history of great spiritual awakenings, you discover that sometimes the world stepped into crisis situations immediately after the outpouring. That was the case in Fredericksburg. There are other times, however, when God brings systemic change to a people that actually shifts the nation into a place of alignment with God, which mitigates and minimizes the crisis that is bearing down upon them.

That day under that massive tent, Allen invited us to seek God's face in such a way that the nation would turn. I've rarely seen a passion for prayer hit a group of people like it did that day in the straw and dirt under our massive tent when Allen was walking out in real time the reality of a father longing for his son to return. As soon as Allen was done speaking, he got word that his son had been found.

If you were a parent and your son or daughter was about to run into the path of a semitruck, it would be loving in that moment for you to shout loudly about the reality of the danger your child was unknowingly stepping into. That is what God is doing right now with us. I'm convinced that the coming move of God will be a dance of joy, but there is also an urgency in the midst of it for lost sons and daughters to return to the Lord.

Repentance means to turn away from our ways and from

our sin and run to Jesus. To turn from your wicked ways is not a call to fix yourself, because we are actually unable to do so. To repent is not a call to grit your teeth and try harder in your own strength and ability. To repent is not to beat yourself up and feel hopeless. To repent is to recognize that you and I need this thing called mercy that is found only in Christ. To repent is to recognize something is really wrong, and we must turn from the way we've been living, declare war on the cancer of sin that's eating up our hearts and relationships, and say yes to Jesus with 100 percent of our wills.

God is the one who changes us. But the change happens in the context of our choices to say yes to Jesus even when that's not the easiest path to take. As I write this, I am aware that some people think love means letting people do whatever they want. They think it's unloving to tell people they need to change almost anything about themselves. But the problem is that this worldly belief is not the true definition of love. The prescription Jesus gives us is so simple and so compelling: return to Him.

Isaiah 30:15 says, "In repentance and rest is your salvation, in quietness and trust is your strength." This means that if you will turn, if you close one door and open the other, if as an act of your will you say, "I am going to declare war and close the door to living in a way that destroys myself and others, and I'm going to turn to love God and say yes to Him," your heart will be refreshed, and you will be able to breathe again. I'm talking about deep, restful breaths. You will be able to breathe because you will be home. You will be covered. Mercy will win. There is a way out.

I WILL FORGIVE THEIR SIN AND WILL HEAL THEIR LAND

I think it's time to sing to our land. I think it's time to dream God's dream for our communities, our nation, and the world.

God wants to heal, not destroy, our land. That has always been and will continue to be His desire. We will receive the fullness of healing when Jesus is standing on the earth again. Although we experience this healing now in significant measure, our desire for this fullness is part of why we long for Him.

When I've observed movements of spiritual awakening beginning to emerge all over the world—in Brazil, Africa, China, Indonesia, Iran, and the Middle East—I am simultaneously thrilled and seriously sobered. I believe the movement I have watched God begin will only continue. God is going to bring miraculous transformation in lives and in the earth as believers host Jesus' presence in churches, on college campuses, and in city streets. I have great anticipation that this Jesus movement is going to crescendo in our generation to a place that is even beyond what eyes have seen and ears have heard (1 Cor. 2:9).

But that doesn't mean life will get easier. Challenges will continue. Things are not guaranteed to get easier, but they *are* guaranteed to get more glorious and even more joyful as we embrace the absolutely clear prescription God gave us in His Word. Second Chronicles 7:14 is God's way back to health for you as an individual, for your community and family, and for nations. But the transformation doesn't start "out there"—it starts in you.

Chapter 17

DISCOVERING YOUR PART IN THE STORY

Where there is no vision, the people perish.
—PROVERBS 29:18, KJV

ONE OF MY primary prayers for you as you read these pages and engage with the concepts in this book is that you would embark on a fresh journey of discovering your part in Jesus' grand story. I hope you are convinced that you have an essential part to play and discovering this role is one of the greatest adventures of your life. There is space for everyone at the table in Jesus' house. In the mystery of God we can all do exploits with Him at the same time and without competition. Some of our exploits will be visible to others; however, most will not. Whether seen or unseen, these exploits are equally significant, powerful, and life changing.

How then can you find your part in this eternal story? There is no formula, but I have identified four specific values that mark those who host Jesus' presence.

VALUE ONE: MINISTRY TO THE LORD

To minister to the Lord is to cultivate the worshipping, praying, David's-tent culture we have been discussing throughout this book. It is when we choose to be Neverites. Ministry to the Lord, at its core, is adoring Jesus in songs and with our affections, speaking back to Him what He has revealed about Himself. It involves asking Him for things, and it involves hearing His voice with a community. This is ministry to the Lord. This was the lifestyle shown in the Book of Acts. I believe worship and prayer are central values for hosting the Lord's presence because they lead us to directly interact with God, and He is the answer to every question.

Imagine if the body of believers actually believed this—if we lived focused on the one thing, which is being in Jesus' presence, and everything else came after it? As challenging as this is to the natural way of thinking, I believe God is looking for people, especially leaders, who will pursue this value with their whole hearts. But no one can do this alone.

Value Two: Community

When Jesus said in Matthew 18:20 that He would live in the midst of those who gather in His name, He was speaking about so much more than physical proximity. In the previous verse Jesus said, "Again, truly I tell you that if two of you on earth agree about anything they ask for, it will be done for them by my Father in heaven" (Matt. 18:19). This is not talking simply about agreement on concepts or ideas. It is painting a picture of the body of believers joining together as if with interlocking parts, where there is love for one another and a shared mission.

I want to brag on our local church, Awakening Community Church. When our team planted the Prayer Furnace, we never planned to start a church. But after years of leading prayer gatherings and internships, things were changing. We planted this church after much prayer and counsel because we felt strongly that we needed a community that would disciple people to walk out the values I'm sharing here as families and individuals.

I think leading Awakening Community Church has been one of the great experiments of my life, and the best is yet to come. Everyone should find a spiritual family. C. S. Lewis wrote, "Next to the Blessed Sacrament itself, your neighbour is the holiest object presented to your senses."[1]

VALUE THREE: MISSIONS AND JUSTICE

Jesus' final words before He ascended to heaven are commonly known as the Great Commission:

> Therefore go and make disciples of all nations, baptizing them in the name of the Father and of the Son and of the Holy Spirit, and teaching them to obey everything I have commanded you. And surely I am with you always, to the very end of the age.
> —MATTHEW 28:19–20

The thing I love about the Great Commission is that Jesus said, "I am with you always." What this says to me is that Jesus is present as we walk in compassion, proclaim the gospel, and engage in acts of justice. As we make prayer and worship a lifestyle, Jesus is right there with us as we are showing Him to those around us.

When the Holy Spirit descended on those assembled in the Upper Room on the day of Pentecost, His presence was for them, but it wasn't only for them. It was also for those who were gathered in Jerusalem from around the world for the Feast of Pentecost. It was for the downtrodden, the broken, the oppressed, and the lost. It was for their neighbors, and the same is true in our day.

It is only by giving away all that God has poured into us that we are able to step into the more that God has for us. It is like breathing in and out. We breathe in when we commune with Jesus; we breathe out when we pour into others through gospel proclamation and acts of compassion and justice. Sometimes one of the reasons we are not able to breathe in more is that we need to breathe out first. We need to give what we've received.

We were designed to function this way. Everything we receive is meant to be given away. We must breathe in, and we must breathe out.

Value Four: Total Obedience

David said in Psalm 101, "I will sing of your love and justice; to you, LORD, I will sing praise. I will be careful to lead a blameless life—when will you come to me?" (vv. 1–2). God is looking to come to people who are fully given to Him, as He is fully given to us.

First John 5:3 says, "This is love for God: to keep his commands." As we discussed in chapter 9, many blessings are reserved for those in total obedience to God because He loves us so much and doesn't want what is meant to bless us to actually hurt us. Jesus makes His presence known to those whose hearts are fully submitted to Him.

An Uncommon Season

The last thing we want to do is simply run events. As helpful as certain kinds of events can be, the Great Commission instructs us to "make disciples." Your voice matters in Jesus' movement. Sometimes the most effective way to find your voice and discover the part you've been called to play is to take an uncommon season to invest in encountering Jesus.

There are training tools for any pursuit people take seriously. Whether it's working with a health coach, going to medical school, or attending football practice multiple days per week for years, when we invest our time and focus in something, we will grow in that area. The same is true of building intimacy with Jesus and discovering your part in His story. No investment is more important because knowing Jesus affects every area of your life.

For years our Awaken the Dawn team had a dream in our

hearts to create an environment where the next generation could spend a year or more—perhaps a gap year—and invest in experiencing the real Jesus, receive biblical training, live in a community centered in the presence of God, and discover their part in His grand story. In 2020 Revive School launched for this very purpose.

It is more important than ever that young adults get connected to Jesus and launched into their destinies. Some students spend the year between high school and college at Revive School. Others use their time here to prepare for a season of full-time ministry. Still others use it to launch into a career. Our dream was that students would be able to spend time every day in worship and prayer, live with others giving their whole lives for Jesus' glory, travel with Awaken the Dawn's big tent, have a front-row seat to the move of God currently taking place in America, and train with nationally known Bible teachers. That is exactly what is happening now as students get hands-on equipping in tracks such as media, worship, missions, and leadership.

I had been praying for years about developing this kind of launching pad, but we needed God to send someone specifically called to lead in this area. I told God, "I know this is something You want in our Awaken the Dawn movement, but who will lead it? I am asking You to send the leader for this training school." We began praying this regularly.

Months later I got a text message from a dynamic young pastor in our region named Jeremy Duggins. We met at a local coffee shop.

God had spoken to Jeremy, seemingly out of left field, when he was on a trip to Bethel Church seeking God for direction and refreshing after years of intense ministry. It was a complete surprise when God spoke to him about leading a training school in Fredericksburg, Virginia. But it was one of the clearest things God had ever spoken to him.

He and his wife, Erica, knew they needed to step out and pursue this but did not know how the word would manifest. I was amazed as he spoke, and I shared with him that we were actually trying to start a training school like the one he had described. We discussed how we could try to collaborate somehow.

After meeting a few times, we realized the school we were praying and dreaming about and the school God had spoken to Jeremy about were the same school. God joined us powerfully. This is often how God will do these things. We found ourselves together in Jesus' story, and out of it has come a friendship and partnership that brings life and strength to each of us.

What Jeremy didn't tell me when we first met early in 2019 was that God had spoken to him that he would be announcing the school on New Year's Eve 2019 at our gathering called Movement 2020. Through a series of events, Jeremy announced the school at that exact time, and we found ourselves, once again, walking out a vision that was beyond our ability to contrive.

Be Part of Something Bigger

Together we can see the presence of Jesus transform our nation and the world. God may be calling you to lead 24/7 prayer and worship in your community. Or He may have you join in with what we've started in Fredericksburg. Or He may be calling you to spend a year at Revive School to help you find your voice and your place in Jesus' movement.[2] At Awaken the Dawn we want to support those seeking to host the presence of Jesus, and God has given us various ways to do that.

Can you imagine tens of thousands of tents filled with public worship, music, prayer, and gospel proclamation covering America with the presence of God and the gospel? I believe thousands of tents covering America would be like a silver bullet for spiritual awakening and for Jesus' worth to go viral. Tent America, a ministry of Awaken the Dawn, is building toward this reality. You can host a tent of 24/7 worship, prayer, and gospel proclamation anywhere—on a college campus, at a church, in a major city. If you are stirred for this and want to host a tent, you can sign up on our website, awakenthedawn. com, and we will send you resources to equip you to host a gathering and put your event on our online portal/map.

We also are taking our massive tent across the nation as a resource. Our passion is to see a move of God sweep our cities, and we want to be a resource that serves and supports what God is already doing with all our hearts.

And finally, to help foster a sense of family and community, we are building a decentralized network called the Awaken the Dawn Leadership Network to connect leaders who have a shared desire to host the presence of Jesus. The leaders in this network will serve in their respective regions and carry this value everywhere. We have regional and state reps to serve those in their regions. We are not asking anyone to leave their organizations and join ours. Our hope is to offer relational connection and discipleship resources to leaders from different movements who share this value of hosting Jesus' presence. As you can see, our annual gatherings and tent events are just part of our heart to help see powerful transformation. Let's come together to see this value for Jesus' presence go viral!

It's Only Beginning

I believe we have only just begun. I am so confident in where the Lord is taking us as the church in the earth. That confidence today is not in our great planning and execution but in the promises of God that are as sure as the sun rises.

We are daring to believe that what David modeled in his tent and what the early church expressed is still the key today. The presence of Jesus changes everything.

This is not about us. This movement of hosting Jesus is going to move far beyond any of us. And for those who have ears to hear, it will bring heaven to earth and transformation to cities, churches, college campuses, and even nations! The Jesus movement is not canceled, and you are a part of it.

FELLOWSHIP PRAYER LIST

A PRAYER LIST IS a simple tool that helps us to focus in our prayer times. Below is a prayer list Mike Bickle developed using the word FELLOWSHIP that is designed to strengthen believers with might in the inner man (Eph. 3:16). You can pray through it every day, as all ten requests are based on promises or prayers in Scripture. The following summary of what each letter in the acronym stands for is drawn from Mike Bickle's book *Growing in Prayer.*[1]

F: Fear of God

The Lord promised that He would put His fear into the hearts of His people: "I will put My fear in their hearts so that they will not depart from Me" (Jer. 32:40, NKJV). He will do this much and more if we ask. As we ask the Holy Spirit to impart the fear of God to our hearts, He unites our hearts to His heart in a way that causes us to have great awe of God (Ps. 86:11). It is far easier to resist sin and compromise when we feel even a small measure of the fear, or awe, of God in our hearts. I ask Him to cause me to delight in the fear of the Lord (Isa. 11:3), and I recommend that you ask Him to strike your heart with the majesty and awesome dread of God according to Isaiah 8:13, "The LORD of hosts, Him you shall hallow; let Him be your fear, and let Him be your dread" (NKJV).

E: Endurance

In the New Testament the words *endurance, perseverance,* and *patience* are often interchangeable. These words speak of being faithful in our God-given assignments and refusing to quit even when facing great pressures. The word *patience* means more than being kind to someone who is disturbing you or patiently listening to someone. Holy Spirit–empowered endurance enables us to seek and serve the Lord faithfully with all our strength for decades without drawing back.

Remember to ask the Holy Spirit to impart endurance to you on the days that you commit to fast. David and Jesus spoke of being consumed with zeal for God's house (Ps. 69:9; John 2:17). One way to ask for endurance is by asking God to impart zeal to your heart. Zeal and endurance are two sides of one coin. It takes God's power touching our hearts and minds to keep us from drawing back in our zeal and wholeheartedness. Ask the Lord to give you endurance or zeal to be faithful especially in the difficult and dry seasons of life.

L: Love

The Holy Spirit's first agenda is to establish the first commandment in first place in the lives of believers so that we will love Jesus with all our hearts and strength. The command to love with all our hearts does not start with us but with God's love for His Son and His people. In fact Jesus asked the Father to impart the very love that He has for Jesus into the hearts of those who long for it (John 17:26). It takes God to love God. The grace to receive God's love and to love Him back is the greatest gift the Spirit imparts to us.

Paul prayed that love would abound in the church (Phil. 1:9). When we ask for our hearts to abound in love, we are actually asking for the Holy Spirit to inspire us in four ways. First, we are asking for greater understanding of God's love for us to abound in our hearts. Second, we are asking the Spirit to tenderize our hearts so that we abound in love for Jesus. Third, we are asking the Spirit to cause love for others to abound in our hearts. Fourth, we are asking the Spirit to help us abound in the same love for ourselves that God has for us. Jesus commands us, "Love your neighbor as yourself" (Matt. 22:39). One reason people hate their neighbors is that they hate themselves. When we see ourselves in the way that God sees us in Christ, we can abound in love even for ourselves in the grace of God.

L: Light of glory

On the day of Paul's dramatic conversion he saw Jesus and His glory in a great light from heaven. Paul recounts the story in Acts 22:6–11. As one who zealously persecuted the followers of Jesus, even condemning them to death, he came face to face with Jesus on the road to Damascus, when "suddenly a great light from heaven shone around [him]" (v. 6, NKJV). Moses prayed, "Please, show me Your glory" (Exod. 33:18, NKJV). Afterward his face shone with the light of glory.

Like Moses we can ask to encounter the realm of God's glory. Jesus spoke of an open heaven in which His disciples would see the angels ascending and descending (John 1:51). Ask Him to shine the light of His countenance on your heart in such a way that you experience the supernatural realm of His glory, including receiving dreams and visions and seeing angels and so on.

O: One thing

It is essential to spend quality time with the Lord in His Word—to be a man or woman of "one thing" as King David was. David revealed his primary life focus when he prayed: "One thing I have desired of the LORD, that will I seek: that I may dwell in the house of the LORD all the days of my life, to behold the beauty of the LORD, and to inquire in His temple" (Ps. 27:4, NKJV).

Another inspiring example is Mary of Bethany, who "sat at Jesus' feet and heard His word" (Luke 10:39, NKJV), while her sister, Martha, was "distracted with much serving" (v. 40, NKJV). Jesus explained to Martha, "One thing is needed, and Mary has chosen that good part" (v. 42, NKJV). We must intentionally set our hearts to be a person of one thing. Ask the Holy

Spirit to help you not to lose this focus by reminding you and intervening to speak to your heart when you start to drift away from the one-thing lifestyle. Ask Him to speak to you about it using Scripture, others, dreams, or His still, small voice to your heart. As I pray this prayer regularly, I become far more sensitized to receiving the Lord's help in the times when I begin to lose my one-thing focus.

W: Worthy

Paul wrote, "We also pray always...that our God would count you worthy of this calling, and fulfill all...His goodness" (2 Thess. 1:11, NKJV). Paul always prayed this for the saints because he understood how important this prayer request is. Walking worthy before the Lord in this passage is not the same as seeking to be worthy by earning our forgiveness. Rather it is about experiencing the grace of God in such a consistent way that we walk with a worthy response to God that prepares us to walk in the fullness of our callings, referred to as "[fulfilling]... all His goodness."

Too many believers come up short of what God has invited them to walk in because of their halfhearted responses and choices. Jesus exhorted us to pray that our responses to Him be esteemed worthy of Him, thus strengthening us to *escape the snare of stumbling* and to stand in victory before Him (Luke 21:34–36). Walking worthy of His leadership and of our callings includes being strengthened to escape the snare of compromise so that we stand in victory before God.

S: Speech

Speech is a very significant issue in our spiritual lives. When our speech comes under the leadership of the Holy Spirit, our entire inner man will also come under His leadership. James tells us, "If anyone does not stumble in word, he is a perfect man, able also to bridle the whole body" (Jas. 3:2, NKJV). Paul exhorted the saints not to speak any corrupt words or to grieve the Holy Spirit by filthy or foolish speech (Eph. 4:29–30; 5:4).

The subject of speech was also on David's prayer list—he asked the Lord to help him control the words of his mouth so that they would be pleasing to God. I encourage you to pray David's prayer often, even on a daily basis: "Let the words of my mouth and the meditation of my heart be acceptable in Your sight, O Lord, my strength and my Redeemer" (Ps. 19:14, nkjv). David purposed that he would not sin with his speech. He asked the Lord to set a guard over his mouth (Ps. 17:3; 141:3).

H: Humility

Jesus called us to learn from Him about walking in humility, or lowliness of heart (Matt. 11:29). He is willing to teach us about this vital subject if we ask Him for understanding. Ask Him to teach you how to walk in humility. Oh, the glory and wisdom of learning humility from Jesus! Paul called us to let the mind of Christ, or His mindset of humility, be in us (Phil. 2:3–5).

I: Insight

The Spirit came to teach us all things—to give us insight or wisdom as He fills us with the knowledge of His will for every area of our lives so we are able to walk in partnership with His heart (Col. 1:9–10). The Lord's desire is to give His people wisdom so that they are fruitful in every endeavor to obey Him and that they grow in or experience the knowledge of His heart in the process. The insight that He gives His people is intended to lead and teach us how to walk in agreement with His heart so that we enjoy deep friendship and partnership with Him. He gives wisdom about how to steward time, money, careers, ministry, health, relationships, and so on. He will give us insight into what is on His heart for our cities, nations, and generations.

P: Peace and joy

The Holy Spirit desires to guard our hearts and minds with supernatural peace; we have only to ask Him. In Philippians 4:7 the heart speaks of our emotions. It is the inheritance of every believer to live in peace. We do not have to live with hearts that are troubled by jealousy, rejection, anxiety, or fear, or with minds that are filled with turmoil, confusion, and indecision. If we regularly ask for peace and joy in specific areas of our lives, we will receive more of them.

PRAYERS TO RECEIVE STRENGTH IN THE INNER MAN USING THE ACRONYM FELLOWSHIP

F—Fear of God: Father, release the spirit of the fear of God into my heart (Ps. 86:11).

E—Endurance: Strengthen my spirit with endurance to do Your will (Col. 1:11).

L—Love: Father, pour out Your love in my heart in a greater measure (Phil. 1:9).

L—Light of glory: Father, let me see more of the light of Your glory (Acts 22:6–11; Exod. 33:18; Ps. 4:6).

O—One thing: In my life focus, I choose to be a person of one thing who sits at Your feet (Ps. 27:4).

W—Worthy: Strengthen me to have a worthy response to God in my life (2 Thess. 1:11).

S—Speech: Father, set a guard over my lips that I may walk free from unclean speech (Eph. 4:29; Ps. 141:3).

H—Humility: Jesus, I want to learn from You how to walk with a lowly heart (Matt. 11:29).

I—Insight (wisdom): Give me insight into Your Word, will, and ways (Col. 1:9–10).

P—Peace and joy: Strengthen my heart with peace and joy that overpower fear (Phil. 4:7).

QUESTIONS FOR STUDY AND PERSONAL GROWTH

THE FOLLOWING QUESTIONS are designed to help you dig deeper into the content of the book and begin the journey of hosting the presence of Jesus.

1. Based on what you read in this book, how would you define the presence of Jesus? How does this understanding affect your expectation of what He wants to do in and through your life?

2. Read Psalm 27:4. What does it mean to you to live a "one thing" life?

3. What does it mean to be a priest in the New Testament? How are you walking this calling out in your life and in your community?

4. Sometimes God will speak creatively in dreams. Describe what you believe the Holy Spirit was referencing when the term Neverite was used in the dream referenced in this chapter.

5. How does it make you feel to know the Father loves you as He loves Jesus? What are some ways we as Christ followers can grow in our love for God?

6. God is always moving. What are some key things God is doing in your region and community, and how can you cooperate with Him in accomplishing these things?

7. What would you do if you could live with a free heart, no longer worrying about your reputation or how you will fund what God has called you to do? What would your life look like if you believed you could "count on [Jesus] continually," as Rolland Baker described?

8. What does the call to total surrender look like in your life in this season? Why is surrender important?

9. What would a great awakening look like in America? How do you envision this taking shape?

10. What is the Lord speaking to you about the part He wants you to play in the story He is writing in the earth?

11. How has the story of *Awaken the Dawn* personally inspired you?

12. How do you believe you are to personally respond to the invitation to host Jesus' presence through building worship and prayer into your personal life and your community?

Personal Application Activities

These are a few action steps you can take to develop a lifestyle of prayer and worship.

1. If it's hard for you to believe God loves you and invites you into the same love the Father has for the Son, meditate on scriptures such as Romans 5:5, Romans 8:35–39, Ephesians 1:5, Ephesians 2:4–5, Ephesians 3:18–19, and 1 John 3:1. Study

them and use them as prayers. You may also want to write in a journal what the Holy Spirit speaks to you from the verses. As you do this regularly, these truths will begin to take root in your heart.

2. Following the encouragement given in chapter 3, write a personal prayer list. Include devotional prayers (prayers focused on intimacy with God) and intercessory prayers (prayers for others or key issues of justice). And don't forget to be thankful!

3. Write down three to five of the primary things you believe God has revealed to you about your calling and assignment to participate in what God is doing in this generation. Begin to regularly pray through these assignments.

4. Write down three biblical passages that speak to what God wants to do in your life, church, campus, workplace, city, and/or nation. Pray those scriptures regularly, and thank God that His Word will not return void but will accomplish that for which it was sent (Isa. 55:11).

NOTES

CHAPTER 1

1. Pete Greig, *Dirty Glory: Go Where Your Best Prayers Take You* (Colorado Springs, CO: Navpress, 2016), 34–35, https://www.amazon.com/Dirty-Glory-Where-Prayers-Chronicles/dp/1631466151?language=en_US.

CHAPTER 2

1. C. S. Lewis, *The Weight of Glory* (San Francisco: HarperCollins, 2001), 25–26, quoted in "What Do You Desire?," C. S. Lewis Institute, December 2004, https://www.cslewisinstitute.org/What_Do_You_Desire.

2. Kevin Prosch, "Endlessness," Palanquin, Forerunner Music, 2013.

CHAPTER 3

1. John Piper, *Desiring God* (Sisters, OR: Multnomah, 1996), 19, https://archive.org/details/desiringgodmedit00pipe_0/page/n5/mode/2up?.

CHAPTER 6

1. Hans Urs von Balthasar, *Prayer*, trans. Graham Harrison (San Francisco: Ignatius Press, 1986), chapter 1, https://www.google.com/books/edition/Prayer/QBgGqL7axgAC?hl=en&gbpv=0.

2. Henri J. M. Nouwen, "God Longs to Bring Me Home," Henri Nouwen Society, January 14, 2021, https://henrinouwen.org/meditation/god-longs-to-bring-me-home/.

3. Teresa of Avila, *The Book of Her Life*, trans. Kieran Kavanaugh and Otilio Rodriguez (Indianapolis: Hackett,

2008), 95–97, https://www.google.com/books/edition/
The_Book_of_Her_Life/knzU10gi72YC?hl=en&gbpv=0.

4. John Piper, "Doing Missions When Dying Is Gain,"
Desiring God, October 27, 1996, https://www.
desiringgod.org/messages/doing-missions-when-dying-
is-gain.

Chapter 8

1. Rolland and Heidi Baker, *Always Enough* (Grand Rapids,
MI: Chosen Books, 2003), 9, https://www.amazon.
com/Always-Enough-Miraculous-Provision-Children/
dp/0800793617/ref=sr_1_1?dchild=1&keywords=There+is
+always+enough+rolland+and+heidi+baker&qid=161184
6906&sr=8-1.

Chapter 9

1. John Ortberg, *The Life You've Always Wanted* (Grand
Rapids, MI: Zondervan, 2009), 77, https://www.google.
com/books/edition/The_Life_You_ve_Always_
Wanted/jckzhepTtHMC?hl=en&.

Chapter 10

1. James Ryle, "Sons of Thunder," Morningstar
Publications, 1991, https://www.harvestsound.com/sons-
of-thunder-prophecy.

2. Blue Letter Bible, s.v. "*pneumatikos*," accessed March
15, 2021, https://www.blueletterbible.org/lang/Lexicon/
Lexicon.cfm?strongs=G4152&t=KJV; Blue Letter
Bible, s.v. "*ōdē*," accessed March 15, 2021, https://
www.blueletterbible.org/lang/Lexicon/Lexicon.
cfm?strongs=G5603&t=KJV.

Chapter 11

1. Walter Wink, *The Powers That Be: Theology for a New Millennium* (New York: Random House, 1998), 185, https://www.amazon.com/Powers-That-Be-Theology-Millennium/dp/0385487525.

2. E. M. Bounds, *The Works of E. M. Bounds* (Zeeland, MI: Reformed Church Publications, 2009), 112, https://www.amazon.com/Works-M-Bounds/dp/1618980319.

3. David Brainerd, *The Life and Diary of David Brainerd* (Peabody, MA: Hendrickson Publishers, 2006), 36, https://www.google.com/books/edition/The_Life_and_Diary_of_David_Brainerd/0MUCUkI7BooC?q.

Chapter 12

1. Mike Bickle, "Great Change and Revival Are Coming to the Church," Mike Bickle Library, August 23, 2019, https://mikebickle.org/watch/2019_08_23_1900_MB_FC.

2. Henri J. Nouwen, *Reaching Out* (London: HarperCollins, 1996), 9, https://www.google.com/books/edition/Reaching_Out/-XaJr93IljQC?hl=en&gbpv=0.

Chapter 14

1. "Tomorrowland 2021," Festicket, accessed March 16, 2021, https://www.festicket.com/festivals/tomorrowland/#:~:text=The%20world's%20biggest%20dance%20music,the%20Belgium%20town%20of%20Boom.

2. Blue Letter Bible, s.v. "*hālal*," accessed March 17, 2021, https://www.blueletterbible.org/lang/lexicon/lexicon.cfm?t=kjv&strongs=h1984.

Chapter 15

1. "Global Summary," Joshua Project, accessed March 17, 2021, https://joshuaproject.net/.

2. Blue Letter Bible, s.v. *"ekballō,"* accessed March 17, 2021, https://www.blueletterbible.org/lang/Lexicon/Lexicon. cfm?strongs=G1544&t=KJV.

Chapter 16

1. Blue Letter Bible, s.v. *"pānîm,"* accessed March 17, 2021, https://www.blueletterbible.org/lang/Lexicon/Lexicon. cfm?strongs=H6440&t=KJV.

2. Greig, *Dirty Glory*, 35.

Chapter 17

1. C. S. Lewis, *The Weight of Glory* (New York: HarperOne, 1976), 46, https://www.google.com/books/edition/ Weight_of_Glory/WNTT_8NW_qwC?hl=en.

2. For more information about Revive School, visit reviveschool.com.

Appendix A

1. Mike Bickle, *Growing in Prayer* (Lake Mary, FL: Charisma House, 2014), 112–123. Used with permission.